THE KABBALAH OF MONEY

THE

KABBALAH

OF

MONEY

*Jewish Insights on Giving,
Owning, and Receiving*

RABBI NILTON BONDER

Translated by Adriana Kac

SHAMBHALA
Boston & London
2001

SHAMBHALA PUBLICATIONS, INC.
HORTICULTURAL HALL
300 MASSACHUSETTS AVENUE
BOSTON, MASSACHUSETTS 02115
WWW.SHAMBHALA.COM

© 1996 by Nilton Bonder

Printed in the United States of America
This edition is printed on acid-free paper that
meets the American National Standards
Institute Z39.48 Standard
Distributed in the United States by Random
House, Inc., and in Canada by Random
House of Canada Ltd.

The Library of Congress catalogues the hardcover edition
of this book as follows:
Bonder, Nilton
[cabala do dinheiro. English]
The Kabbalah of Money: insights on livelihood, business,
and all forms of economic behavior / Nilton Bonder.
p. cm.
ISBN 1-57062-214-0 (cloth: alk. paper)
ISBN 1-57062-804-1 (pbk.)
1. Judaism—Economic aspects. 2. Judaism and social problems.
3. Economics—Religious aspects—Judaism. 4. Ethics, Jewish.
I. Title.
BM509.E27B6613   1996   96-14964
296.3'85644—dc20   CIP

Contents

CONTENTS

CONTENTS

CONTENTS

THE KABBALAH OF MONEY

where we stand within the immense Market of values that we call reality. This is the Market of exchanges and interactions of all kinds from which we have learned to derive the concept of economic markets. It represents the infinite quantity of small and great businesses that take place in the universe at any given moment. These businesses are made possible through the mediation of an incredible diversity of "currencies." These "moneys," which can be studied through the model of our ordinary, daily money, are the main focus of this book.

Jewish tradition has much to contribute to this inquiry. Jews have had their image stereotypically attached to the love of money. They've seen their patriarchs—Abraham, Isaac, and Jacob—turned into the main characters of jokes about stinginess and greed. Their greatest symbol of impurity, the pig, has been mockingly promoted to best friend in the form of a piggy bank. They have been caricatured with long noses, presumed to guide them through the gutters of our financial systems.

I will avoid making apologies, which would inevitably lead to an admission of bias on my part. But I would like to invite the objective reader who is familiar with the bypaths of this world to share a less judgmental analysis. I speak to those who recognize that over and above considerations of good and evil, human experience is distinguished by the constant adjustment of our intentions as they come into contact with reality. Our capacity to transform experience into culture and tradition allows future generations to relate to a fixed body of morals and ethics, which they can develop, criticize, and improve. This process leads us to self-knowledge of our own humanity.

In a way, Jews are indispensable to the collective memory of the West. Upon them the West projects many of its social fantasies, as well as many of civilization's sublimated and repressed experiences, which tend to manifest in those perceived as being "other."

In fact, the "negative" characteristics projected onto Jews are often revealing of their cultural efforts towards behaviors that are the very opposite of these stereotypes. People often fantasize about the rabbi who eats pork behind the closed doors of the temple, or the priest who holds secret trysts in the confession booth, or the politician who conducts fraudulent transactions from the basement of the senate. We betray, with these thoughts, the great burden placed upon those whose task it is, at least nominally, to challenge our animal instincts and reactions. In other words, culture (which challenges us in precisely this way) creates in us a desire for its own collapse, for the unmasking of its anti-human theoretical propositions of right and wrong, construction and destruction.

Jews, as creators and promoters of what was to become the ethical heritage of the West, fell prey to a reaction against the restrictions it imposed on human behavior. They originated the fundamental law "Thou shalt not kill," and yet they are charged with *the* great historical "murder." The Jews of the Middle Ages—a period of urbanization characterized by a disregard for

hygienic and sanitary concerns—whose traditional customs were known exactly for their hygienic content, are
nevertheless depicted as filthy and rejoicing in their
filth. Despite being bound by severe dietary prescrip-
tions, they are accused of cannibalistic rituals involving
Christian children. And finally, Jews are saddled with a
reputation for being obsessive about money. Their God,
of whom they are not permitted to make images, is assigned the shape of a dollar sign. And yet it is true that
the Jews respect money; for in it they see a content
which speaks of the true distance between the heart and
the pocket.

The deeper meaning of money—and, in the
broader sense, of earning a living (*parnasah*, livelihood)—is dealt with in Jewish tradition both ethically
and with courageous humanity. *The Kabbalah of Money*
is an offering of rabbinical and mystical insights into an
ecology of money, involving the health of all forms of
exchange, transaction, and interdependence. In it, we
will take "Kabbalah" to be above all a methodology for
understanding in a profound way things that appear to
be superficial, uncovering hitherto unrealized dimensions of our everyday reality. We will be broadly referring to "the rabbis" (including the commentators cited
in the Talmud as well as legendary figures of the
Ḥasidic world) as the keepers of a method of interpreta-
tion which understands reality as having multilayered
dimensions. The "peeling" of those dimensions, from
the most manifest and evident to those which are hidden and occult, is what came to be known as Kabbalah.

Literally the term comes from the root verb "to receive" *(kibel)*, and it hints at the ancient tradition passed on and received from generation to generation. In its most basic reduction, it proposes that through the simple we can get to the complex; from the concrete to the abstract; from the detail to the large picture. Here we will be applying this method to the concept of "money."

The rabbis tell us that through money, we establish day-to-day situations that uncover our bigotry and illusions and expose us in a way only practice and empirical experimentation can otherwise do. We are as we react, we are what we believe, and our money is an extension of our reactions and beliefs. Based on the money that moves in and out of our lives, we structure our comprehension of the world. And this is one of the main factors in determining our understanding of reality: how much things and people are worth to us, and how much we are worth to them.

The rabbis, after thoroughly analyzing money, have chosen to treat it in much the same way as they consider our bodily existence. They recognize, without overlooking the importance of the soul and of intention, that the true reality of the body is an indispensable tool in understanding who we are and what path we should take in life.

I therefore invite the reader to stroll through the familiar world of the pocket. I propose a tour through this world of Markets, a journey into the shadows cast by money on emotional and spiritual dimensions. We shall look at our exchanges in such a way that the dark shadow of our souls is cast off from our money, and we come to accept our human limits of wealth.

In reality, money is usually seen as something dirty that we are ashamed to talk about. People have less trouble telling friends about intimate sexual matters than they have in sharing the size of their bank accounts or their salaries. Children very rarely know how much their parents earn.

Yet money is not something evil. The Spanish philosopher Ibn Zabara asked, "What is the cause of death? Life itself." Similarly, we may ask: "What is the cause of money?" The answer is that it has not come into existence as a means of oppression or an instrument of greed; rather, money—surprisingly—arises from the human desire for justice and the hope for a better world. Over time, money has absorbed fundamental traces of human nature that can now be understood by paying close attention to the values we attach to it and its symbolism.

Yes, Jews respect money—real (that is, uncorrupted) money that multiplies the possibilities of livelihood and frees up their time for spiritual study, for learning. And they know that this kind of learning is like sap: it is life itself.

What kind of money is this that can be the topic of sacred writings? What kind of money is this that religious people busy themselves with it? What money is this that can also be used as currency in the world-to-come or in paradise? How should we deal with a Market of existence that underprices meanings and deflates our

THE KABBALAH OF MONEY

time and values, while at the same time inflating our dissatisfaction and bringing on a recession of our potential? The rabbis have proposed answers to some of these questions in their search for a "strong currency."

"Let's Make a Deal"

> Whoever wishes to live in sanctity, may he live according to the true laws of commerce and finance.
> —*Babylonian Talmud, Bava Kama* 30a

"Let's do a *gesheft*"—let's make a deal—are words that, when pronounced on earth, trigger great commotion in Heaven. It is a sacred moment when two individuals establish an exchange in good conscience and optimize gain for both parties. Doing business in the world as imagined by the rabbis puts to the test all our efforts towards culture, spirituality, and individual responsibility where it extends beyond our own needs to others. Only two just people can embark on a *gesheft*, not avoiding it out of cowardice and emerging from it with maximum gain for each relative to the maximum gain of the other and the minimal loss to the universe. This type of transaction, which presupposes the nonpredatory use of resources and the fulfillment of the needs of all participants, establishes a new kind of Nature: a natural order in which we are not merely subject to external chaos or to casual survival. It is a Nature where survival is not determined merely by genetic fitness and where our sense of justice and our discerning wisdom introduce a sacred dimension into reality. This new kind of Nature I have designated as the "Market." The less developed it is in the rabbinical sense, the closer the Market will be to primitive nature—that is, to a wilderness. The Market is, therefore, where each individual's fitness to survive is in accordance with his or her own perception of what survival is. Survival is the ability to support ourselves physically and live up to our responsibilities. These responsibilities are fundamental so that exchanges may be made within a rabbinical Market and not within nature. The infiltration of immediate interests that have not been restrained by responsibilities poisons the Market and contributes to the chaotic possibilities that can befall us. So strong is this rabbinical concept of likeness between Market and Nature, despite their essential differences, that the following story is told:

A very righteous rabbi was allowed to visit both purgatory (Gehenna) and paradise (Gan Eden, the Garden of Eden). First he was taken to purgatory, where he heard terrible screams coming from the most tormented beings he had ever seen. As he drew near, he saw that they were seated at a large banquet table set with the most exquisite silverware and china and laden with the most delicious foods imaginable. Unable to understand why these people suffered so much, the rabbi looked closer and saw that their elbows were inverted, so that they could not bend their arms and bring the food to their mouths.

The rabbi was then taken to paradise, where he

heard laughter and sensed a joyous, celebratory atmosphere. However, to his astonishment, he came upon
the exact same scene, with people sitting at a sumptu-
ous banquet table laden with the same delicacies he
had seen before—everything was the same, including
their inverted elbows. Only one detail was different:
each person brought food to his or her neighbor's
mouth.

Purgatory is a world with no Market, where a certain difficulty is enough to destroy our ability to enjoy
the banquet. In paradise, besides the pleasure of the
delicacies we enjoy, we soothe our frustration each time
we bring food to our neighbor's mouth. However, it is
important to perceive that both purgatory and paradise,
Market and Nature, can be taken externally for the
same situation. The gap between getting this insight of
feeding one another and not catching on to it is very
great. We confront this gap every day of our lives.

Real Money versus Money as Frozen Work

In the popular collection of rabbinical sayings known
as *The Ethics of the Fathers (Pirkei Avot)*, we read:
"Where there is no flour, there is no Torah. Where there
is no Torah, there is no flour."

The first of these statements is clear enough: when
we cannot get flour—that is, material goods to sustain
ourselves—we cannot be expected to worry about study
and spiritual growth (Torah). The second statement is

not so obvious. It points to the origin of flour—not the flour found in nature, but the flour of the Market. Torah makes the Market feasible by imposing limits upon human needs and upon the acceptable means of satisfying these needs, and by reminding us of the responsibilities inherent in all material transactions.

In speaking of this "flour," we are not talking about just any kind of money or goods, because for the acquisition of goods, Torah is not necessary. Still, all money honestly materialized within the Market, far from Nature, is reason for joy and hope, a sure sign of life. We earn real money through fair exchanges, which optimize the profits for all those directly and indirectly involved. As the One God is the universal guardian of fairness, real money is guaranteed by God: it is "realizable" within the cosmos.

What is money, after all? Money is an important symbol of an agreement—one that implies that we all wish to live in paradise as described in the story. This agreement was consolidated through humanity's first experiences of exchange, and made way for the emergence of a mode of survival that was so detached from Nature that, in itself, it didn't guarantee survival. Drawing from their early barter experiences, human beings came to trust that a coin made of a rare metal of a certain weight was guaranteed to have the same real value as the chicken for which it was exchanged. A possessor of coins could certainly not consume them for his own survival as he could a chicken, but he knew that he held something of identical value. With time, we began to trust the Market to such an extent that it was possible to substitute for coins that had rarity value, coins that had no value at all. Paper and inferior metals, apart from not having the nutritional value of a chicken, don't even have the same nominal value. These coins carried a promise of ten, fifty, or one thousand units of chicken. This promise was vouched for by the aforementioned agreement, which, with time, became even more assimilated and accepted as the result of a collective desire to create a Market. This promise was vouched for by God.

The two different kinds of symbols of this agreement take their names from the stage of trust in which they emerged.

The first, as a result of its "weight," was given names like *pound, peso,* or *shekel* (literally "weight" in Spanish and in Hebrew), and it weighed the equivalent of the real value of the chicken. The second kind of symbol the rabbis call a *zuz* (derived from a Hebrew root meaning "in movement," "circulating"), a coin of olden times whose weight and real value are not related to the chicken. The *zuz* (plural, *zuzim*) is the currency of the rabbis. Despite having no worth in itself, it is a symbol of humanity's interdependence, of the accepted contract, and of the fact that we all understand the difference between "purgatory" and "paradise." Thus is born the fundamental trust that God vouches for all *zuzim.*

Money, *zuzim,* is not evil in itself. Much to the contrary, it reflects our desire for organization, civilization, peaceful coexistence, and, in the long run, for ecology (in other words, for Torah). This agreement can only exist in an atmosphere of faith. Faith is often idolized as a belief in the institution of investment, in the financial system, in governmental institutions or the State, or as patriotism. But in fact, the agreement can only exist if there is absolute faith. It is not by chance that we find on various currencies of the *zuz* family (which have no inherent value), such as the dollar, the strange phrase "In God We Trust." This is another version of the word *amen*, a Hebrew word related to the word for faith, *emunah*. Some have seen the word *amen* as a Hebrew acronym for the assertion *El Melekh Ne'eman:* God Is a Faithful King. This statement imbues a piece of printed paper with faith and vouches for its value in a transaction. But above all, it should vouch for the fact that the money is real money and represents survival and the responsibilities that go with it—the same responsibilities that conceive a currency as having a value that does not exist for those who are not part of the agreement.

Real money is very different from the money found in nature. To our human perception, the money found in nature could function as an idolatrous element like the golden calf: it can lead us to believe that its value lies within the object itself, rather than in the preservation of the agreement. Preserving the agreement, producing real money, and corresponding to the Market is not an easy task. It is as difficult as bringing on the messianic era, as difficult for us human beings as optimizing our humanity.

The value of real money increases when we tax it with responsibilities that are part of the levels of unity and civility that a community strives for, and its value decreases when we bypass these responsibilities. This depreciation is the cruel fate of every symbol that loses its meaning.

Money is not only the exchange of responsibly taxed goods ("flour"), but also something that is symbolic of work responsibly taxed. To the rabbis, money in this sense is equivalent to "frozen work." Let's say the value of work is x (supply of this work), multiplied by y (units of intellectual difficulty or engineering involved), multiplied by z (physical effort incurred). The end product is hypothetically frozen in the form of money. A unit of money should therefore represent this multiplication in which none of the variables can be zero, lest the value of the money be zero. Neither can they take on values that tend to infinity or soar dangerously high, for there are real limits to the value of any work.

An attempt to make one of these variables tend to infinity creates inflation in the Market (little work and much money). Even when we disproportionately value one of the variables (making it tend to infinity), and another is pressed to values close to zero—thus creating a compensation process whereby the money is generated that is apparently proportional to the work—we must take care not to generate false money. The more developed a community is, the greater is its care in avoiding imbalance between these variables. There is a limit to the quantity of "frozen work" that we can have in the bank—corresponding to the limits placed on our human energy and life span. Therefore, when a society allots the wealth derived from work disproportionately to a single individual, it means that false money has been produced by that society. We shall return to this issue later when we discuss the limits of wealth and livelihood.

Creating Abundance

I've been poor and I've been rich. Believe me, rich is better!

Better rich and healthy than poor and sick.

—Yiddish sayings

The rabbis saw poverty as an unparalleled tragedy. In the *Midrash* (*Exodus Rabbah* 31:14) we read: "Nothing in the universe is worse than poverty; it is the most terrible of sufferings. A person oppressed by poverty is like someone who carries on his shoulders the weight of the whole world's sufferings. If all the pain and all the suffering of this world were placed on one scale and poverty on the other, the balance would tilt towards poverty."

In order to combat this universal enemy, which has both natural and human components, the rabbis developed the concept of *yishuv olam*, the effort of "settling the world." Derived from Genesis 2:15, where human beings are assigned the task "to till and tend" the land, this concept states that we should constantly try, while maintaining an honest relationship with the world, to increase the overall quality of life. It is the duty of every one of us to expand wealth—and not only our own—into the world around us. Let us define wealth as the highest level of organization possible to the environment in such a way that everything alive and everything essential to life exists without scarcity. In other words, the more abundance we create for a given human need, *without generating the scarcity of another need,* the better. This is every person's duty: to improve the quality of life around him or her.

Creating abundance without creating scarcity in this vast universe, which stretches way beyond our human capacity of measurement and judgment, is very difficult. And in case of doubt, it's always better to enjoy nonscarcity rather than abundance. If we transform something into abundance and thereby generate scarcity, we are giving ourselves a double chore: that of creating abundance and that of having to replenish, because of this abundance, whatever has been depleted. As a result of this difficulty, the righteous, when in doubt, chose not to create abundance. However, it is our duty to create maximum abundance for all without generating scarcity. In the language of the rabbinical Market, this is the ideal condition in which "one party doesn't lose, and the other gains." This condition is of utmost importance for any market that aims to grow and enrich the environment. And the righteous are responsible for making this happen. Let's look at an example developed by the rabbis.

According to the Jewish "law of neighbors" *(dina de bar-metzra)*, if a person has land that borders someone else's, the neighbor automatically has first option of acquisition. The selling price must be within the market price for the area, so that there is no loss for the seller and the buyer gains from the transaction because the expansion of his property represents an increase in its value. In this manner, one of the participants gains and the other loses nothing.

Another example of this concept is found in the Talmud (*Ketubot* 103a): Ruben rented his mill to Simon under the condition that the latter would grind his grain for him as payment. Later, however, Ruben became rich and bought another mill where he could grind his grain at no cost. As he no longer needed Simon to grind for him, if he now asked for compensation in money instead of the grinding agreement, Simon could refuse. In the event that Simon had many clients to grind for at his mill, in such a way that with the time and effort needed to grind for Ruben he could grind for another person and not suffer any loss, Simon would be compelled to agree to the payment. This decision is established so that he should not come to behave like the inhabitants of Sodom, who refused to do favors for one another, even at no cost to themselves.

Doing favors is an obligation, and the implications of refusing to do favors are similar to those of theft. If we prevent someone from gaining something, even if we don't derive any gain from it ourselves, we are stealing the potential heritage of humanity. Our responsibility extends to everything we control directly or indirectly; it goes beyond what we own to include what we influence. The act of preventing someone from having something is comparable to taking something away from him. If we obstruct the wealth of the Market around us, we contribute to scarcity and keep the forces of livelihood from materializing. In doing so we are preventing the quality of life from increasing in this immediate cosmos and infringing the law of "settling the world." It is sometimes difficult to realize that the attitude of "One person doesn't lose and another gains" falls into the same category as "One person takes from another."

Acquiring wealth is a human need. And fighting scarcity is essential, as it clears the path for the livelihood guaranteed by God to reach its recipient. But are there restrictions on our activity of enrichment, apart from the requirement not to damage the world by creating some kind of scarcity in the very act of enriching?

2

THE LIMITS OF WEALTH

It's not that having money is so good; it's that not having it is so bad!

—*Yiddish saying*

The sinful cities of Sodom and Gomorrah described in the Book of Genesis represent a society that is sick because it is unable to help itself towards the "settling of the world." In refusing to help one another in such a way that "one doesn't lose and another gains," the citizens of Sodom and Gomorrah created a miserable market, similar to the purgatory described in chapter 1, in which inverted elbows don't cooperate. It is curious, however, that another, apparently different society is charged, also in Genesis, with having the same kind of "sick market." I'm referring to the generation of Babel (Hebrew for Babylon), the ancient city where people tried to build a tower to reach Heaven. As punishment, God scattered them all over the face of the earth.

According to the rabbis, Babel's greatest mistake was transforming social and economic activities into an end in themselves. In this case, even if we have a situation where people with inverted elbows do feed themselves, we can't call it paradise. In our story, one of the great pleasures of paradise was not simply gaining access to the food that was on the table, but the possibility of accomplishing, through this food, something even more pleasurable: exchange. An inverted elbow constantly bringing food to our mouths can be extremely frustrating if the owner of the elbow doesn't know what he's doing and pays no attention to our pace as recipients of the food. We might find ourselves losing our appetite while having spoons and forks insistently poked at us, forcing on us something that as children we experienced as extremely uncomfortable.

When the rabbis try to explain that economic activities can sanctify us, they are referring to the internal mechanism that we use to "uplift" and "instruct" our physical dimension, our own bodies. Reb Shmuel of Sochochov used to say: "The soul does not need spiritual elevation—it is pure. It is the body that needs to be purified by us human beings, because that was the Creator's reason for creating it." Or, as another master used to say: "We don't *have* a soul, we *are* a soul. We *have* a body."

This strange division between "body" and "soul," which sometimes makes sense and sometimes misleads us, can perhaps be transposed to the sphere of pleasure as the difference between "immediate" and "cumulative" pleasure. Satisfying the body is as easy as making it suffer—everything is determined by the speed of our neurons. And if our neurons are the speed limit and the quickest way to generate rewarding experiences (of pleasure or pain), then comparatively, the speed of the experiences of the soul is the slowest possible. Experiences of the soul are only really completed and apparent to us after certain stages of our life have gone by. Experiences of the body easily satiate through repetition and bring on, as a byproduct, an awareness of death. The soul rereads these same experiences and translates them into existence. And existing is extremely pleasurable. Taking on and living up to our responsibilities, we optimize our potential, create wealth, and "settle the world" for the Great Market of the cosmos.

All of this is to say that the enrichment of the body is limited by the enrichment of the soul—and that we should avoid emphasizing bodily experiences at the expense of soul experiences. The rule here is clear: abundance that generates scarcity is a double loss of time.

I have tried to identify ways in which abundance generates scarcity within our experience, or within the limits of wealth, now adding the word "human" to our definition of "wealth." There are limits imposed by time, ecological issues, and moral issues. Let us study these limits in this order, because the first two are more generic, while the third calls for a deeper analysis of the Market and, indirectly, of "money," or exchange.

Wasting Time

It's better to do nothing than to transform something
into nothing.

—*Yiddish saying*

When interpreting the verse of Proverbs (6:6) that
reads, "Go to the ant, O lazy one; study its ways and
learn," the rabbinical commentators explain that the
ants are a symbol of wasted work: "They need only two
grains of wheat to survive the whole season, and yet
they work incessantly to save up a fortune." The question is: what should we learn from this? That is, what
should we do with our time? Much of our accumulation
of wealth is the result of having nothing to do, or nothing better to do. Our mortality and existential questions
drive us, whenever we have free time, to choose to combat scarcity and thus accumulate time for when we do
have something to do. In Jewish tradition the question
of what to do with our time has a standard answer:
study. Time is to be divided between study, work, and
physiological needs (eating, sleeping, elimination,
and leisure). All our free time, once our physiological
and work needs have been fulfilled, should be dedicated to studying. Therefore, work or units of scarcity
converted into abundance have an additional limit
within the physical time limit of human beings.

Let me clarify that what Judaism means by study
is literally the study of the Torah, of those values that
make us more human in our capacity to perceive reality

with insight and to feel compassion for others, understanding them through our own nature. This study pro-
motes the coming of paradise and should be culturally
encouraged. Our culture should teach those who have
not yet fulfilled all their needs that it is not a good idea
to spend all their time trying to satisfy them. We may
consider ourselves different from the generation of the
Tower of Babel, in that we seek to reach the limit of our
needs and *then* propose to begin our studies; but in fact,
like the people of Babel, we commit the error of wasting
time *(bittul zeman)*. Our time has a fundamental purpose, which is to drive us to *be* more and know more
about our potential. The time that we dedicate to other
activities is also time spent on the path of life and of
self-knowledge (which is the reason why the Market
sanctifies it), but this kind of time is subject to real
limits, which, when overstepped, represent an inappro-
priate use of time intended for soul experiences. These
soul experiences, despite being influenced by time
spent on other activities, only come to completion when
we set aside some real time for them. With this in mind,
it is better to do nothing than to transform something
into nothing. It is better to face the emptiness than to
enrich ourselves beyond our own limits and make nothing of our time. Having to deal with this nothingness
drives us to study, the true kind of study that carries no
expectation of personal gain.

Learning for Its Own Sake: Study That Leads to No Personal Gain

Let me add a small parenthesis about studying, as it interferes with our wealth and is a good of utmost importance to the Market. A market contaminated with too much time generated through *bittul zeman* (waste of time, or as we would now say, waste of study time) becomes corroded to the point where the real value of what circulates, decreases. The depression, apathy, and lack of meaning in life that comes with too much wasted time are high prices the Market must pay for this waste. So the big thing for us is to study. But what exactly do we mean by this?

Maimonides said that we humans only develop through our perception of the reward or remuneration associated with studying. As children, we study to earn the reward of candy from the teacher. Later on, we study to receive peanuts. As adolescents, we study thinking about earning a living. As adults, we study to deserve honor and enjoy the respect of others. However, only when we reach maturity do we study with nothing at all in mind.

In Hebrew we say we study *lishmah,* "for its own sake," in order to exist. This is not as strange as it sounds. After all, we must eat, sleep, and work in order to exist. And when we work more than necessary, we produce *bittul zeman,* wasted existence. It also makes sense that if we study and work to create abundance and eliminate scarcity, and if we've already gathered wealth, all our study and all our work, by definition, now aim at nothing at all. If we insist on thinking that the aim of studying and working is wealth beyond its possible limits, then we are insisting on transforming something into nothing.

Why, then, are we compared to the generation of the Tower of Babel when we pursue wealth first, in order to dedicate ourselves later to study "for nothing"? Because this wealth, much like the tower that sought to reach the sky, fails to project into the future. No one can guarantee his or her own wealth in the future, because there is no amount of accumulated wealth that can compensate for scarcity. Therefore, we must help those who have not yet reached maturity and who are still far from any kind of material stability, so that these people understand that they are also required to devote some of their time to study that leads nowhere.

According to Jewish tradition, even our salary is payment for our *bittul zeman* (loss of time that could have been dedicated to studying), so that through our productive work someone else may benefit directly or indirectly from his or her own *zeman* (time set aside for studying). Time is one of the limits imposed upon wealth. Time is money, but not all the time we have should be converted into money.

Ecological and Physical Limits

If wealth is defined as abundance that does not create scarcity, there must be further limits imposed upon this wealth. Livelihood that is preserved in nature should only be transformed into concrete livelihood when it is necessary. There is no better way to store livelihood than in nature. During Israel's exodus out of slavery in Egypt, finding sustenance in the desert was a major problem. The Bible describes how a daily portion (manna) miraculously fell to the ground every morning. When the Hebrews tried to gather more than their daily portion, not only did the surplus spoil, but the environment was also impacted, reducing its desire to promote livelihood. Once again, we see that unless it is necessary, it is better to do nothing than to transform something into nothing. We must be very careful lest our profit be merely apparent. A profit today that will cost us tomorrow is not wealth; much to the contrary, it is a double loss of time. We are often forced to behave like this to survive, but a sophisticated Market should plan to avoid this kind of situation, which goes against the law of *yishuv olam*, settlement of the world.

Who Is Really Rich?

The Talmud says: Who is really rich?

Rabbi Yose used to say: One who has a bathroom near his dining room.

Rabbi Meir used to say: One who derives inner peace from his fortune.

—*Shabbat* 25b

Rabbi Meir draws from common knowledge when he says that the truly rich are those who acquire maximum quality of life without creating scarcity for themselves or others, who live up to their responsibilities, avoid "wasting time," and do not draw livelihood from Nature beyond what is truly necessary. Rabbi Meir called this the "inner peace" derived from one's fortune. In other words, it's not easy to be really rich. We find an interesting description of a false rich man written by Bahya ibn Pakuda in his eleventh-century masterpiece, *Duties of the Heart:*

> He believes that his ideas on financial issues are his most sophisticated thoughts. . . . His dreams drive him to the most incredible expectations, such that his various kinds of property are not enough for him. He is like a fire that burns more intensely as logs are put on. His heart is excited by his dreams. He anxiously awaits the season when the goods must be stored and again the time when they must be sold. He studies the situation of the market, broods over the rise or fall of the prices of goods, and watches how rates vary in different parts of the world. No heat, chill, storm, ocean, or distance can keep him from the most distant places. He does all of this hoping to reach an end, in a situation which in fact has no end and can cause him much pain, tribulation, and wasted effort. And if he does get something of what he hoped for, he will probably be allowed to keep of his fortune only the labor needed to care for it, manage it, and guard it from all sorts of dangers, until it finally winds up in the hands of the person it was destined for.

Being rich is an art that requires the simplicity of never forgetting why we wished to be rich to begin with. At the same time, this requirement does not excuse us from the ideals of wealth, and we must be careful not to exaggerate in this "simplicity." We should adapt our needs to what livelihood is granted us, but not lose sight of the final goal of increasing the quality of life for ourselves and others. "Simple-mindedness" can be harmful to the Market and to the cosmos.

The Yiddish writer I. L. Peretz tells an interesting story about a character that he calls "silent Bontche." Bontche was a simple man who lived a life of no ambitions, going about his business of cleaning the streets. Humble and childless, he never quarreled with anybody, and even in death he was buried as a pauper, without so much as a tombstone. Among the inhabitants of Heaven, however, there was much excitement. Never had they received such a noble soul, and one and all flocked to the celestial court to welcome this pure spirit. The Creator Himself insisted on conducting the trial, and the heavenly prosecutor was furious when he realized he would be arguing a lost cause. Bontche stood before the angels, the Creator, and the prosecutor, who right up front refused to press charges. The Creator then began to speak, commending Bontche and saying to him: "Your life on earth was so wonderful that everything here in Heaven is yours. You have only to ask and you will have anything you want. What do you wish for, O pure soul?"

Bontche looked suspiciously towards the Creator and, taking off his hat, said: "Anything?"

"Anything!" replied the Creator.

"Then I would like some milk and coffee and some bread with a little butter."

At these words, disappointment echoed through the Heavens. The Creator was deeply embarrassed, and the prosecutor made no effort to control his laughter. Bontche was not righteous—he was just simple-minded.

In life, our best is required from us. It's true that this "best" depends upon many variables, but our best is required nonetheless. There is no way out of this. The very definition of life involves knowing how to manage maximum wealth and maximum respect towards the people and things in our environment. This balance not only brings inner peace, but also increases the overall wealth of the Market and improves the world around us.

No One Can Take What's Yours

One day, the pager rang and my secretary's voice said, "Rabbi? There's a young man here who says he's a Kabbalist and wants to speak to you. May I send him up?"

It was not often that a Kabbalist knocked at my door, so I agreed. A calm, solemn figure entered and introduced himself in broken English: "My name is Moishe, I'm a Kabbalist, and I'm here to sell you some books." While he began to display his wares, I surveyed this unusual young man and tried to extract some information from him.

He told me that he had entered the country with a thousand books, which had been seized at the airport. He had nevertheless managed to recover them, despite his lack of import papers and his ignorance of Brazilian law. He said to me: "The difficult part is writing books about Kabbalah. All kinds of bad things happen when one undertakes such work. The 'Other Side' [*sitrah aḥarah*, the side of evil] does everything it can to stop you: the warehouse where you keep your paper catches fire, machinery break down, and so forth. . . . But once the book is printed and bound, and becomes *parnasah* [livelihood], then nothing can be done against you."

As I pondered this idea, Moishe decided to give me the address where he was staying, and to find it he began to empty his pockets, placing various wads of currency notes on my desk. I asked him, "Do you walk around the streets carrying money like that? Don't you know it's dangerous? We have frequent muggings around here." He looked at me with surprise and said, "There is also a rule which says that what is truly yours, no one can take from you . . . if it's *parnasah*, of course."

Later I came to know that Moishe traveled around town by bus to sell the Kabbalistic books he had brought with him. When we met again, I asked him, "How do you manage to sell books in Hebrew to people who can't understand them?" He explained, "I tell them that these books, even if they are difficult to read, are good books to have—that the mere fact of having them on one's shelf invites blessings."

What really touched me was Moishe's deterministic attitude, and the way it reaffirmed that, above all, a great salesman was loose on the streets, struggling for his livelihood. It was obvious to him that a certain amount of livelihood was already guaranteed—and that this livelihood was not dependent upon his conscious effort to sell or earn more.

In Jewish tradition we have a similar of discussion concerning "free will" and *segulah* (literally, "treasure"). Free will is a conscious effort towards obtaining or doing something, while *segulah* is an internal force inherent to the soul and independent of our decision-making. Livelihood is an interaction between these two forces. In the same way that some of the activities necessary to maintain life are active—such as doing, attacking, or escaping—others are passive and take place outside of our consciousness, even though they involve an effort on our part: breathing, digestion, and heartbeat, for example.

According to the rabbis, we all carry with us inbred movements of livelihood: some are active and represent the sum of our conscious efforts; others are passive, like a "treasure" hidden inside our soul, which emerges in the form of luck, say, or a knack for business.

We recognize this with certain kinds of intuition. Experiences of intuition help us to realize that who we are is a result not only of education and formation, but also of "gifts" coming from unknown sources. Through them we can identify resources that we don't have absolute control over, but which are available and accessible to us. One can draw a parallel, for example, with sight or hearing. These two abilities mix sympathetic and parasympathetic responses. We see and hear independently of any conscious control of these senses, but we are able to direct them according to our wishes. In the same way, we can combine our *segulah*, our gift or "parasympathetic" response, with free will, or conscious deliberation, to shape behavior.

What Moishe wanted to say is that our *segulah* cannot be impaired by evil forces, or the "Other Side," while our free will can. Moishe also wanted to point out that *parnasah* cannot be stolen. It's possible to steal *things*, but not livelihood, as livelihood already takes into consideration the possible losses and shadows that may loom over us. Goods and coins can be taken from us, but not livelihood. Likewise, a book that can be interfered with when it is being written becomes immune once it turns into a vehicle of livelihood. We therefore should not let ourselves be set back by disastrous episodes in the history of our *parnasah*. Let us consider the following story told by the great Ḥasidic master Rabbi Naḥman of Bratslav:

In a certain town there lived a poor man who earned his living digging clay, which he sold. One day, while he was digging, he found a precious stone. He tried to have it priced, but he discovered that nobody in his town or in the surrounding towns had enough money to buy it, so great was its value. He thus had to travel to London to have it priced in a suitable market.

Being very poor, the man had to sell everything he had, and with this money he managed to reach the port. Upon arriving there, he realized he wouldn't have enough money to buy a ticket to England. So he found the captain of the ship and showed him the precious stone. The captain was very impressed and let him board the ship, thinking that the owner of such a gem must be a very rich and respectable person. The captain gave him a first-class cabin on the ship, with all the luxuries usually granted to the very rich. The man, now quite satisfied with his accommodations, delighted in his precious stone, especially during meals, as it improves the digestion to eat in a good mood and in high spirits. One day, however, he fell asleep beside his stone as it lay on the table. One of the servants came into the room to clean it and, not noticing the stone, shook the tablecloth outside the window into the sea.

When the man woke up and realized what had happened, he was so desperate that he almost lost his head. What would the captain do to him now that he couldn't pay for the trip and for the accommodations? He would surely be killed. He finally decided to remain in high spirits as if nothing had happened. Recently, the captain had taken to spending a couple of hours a day with this man, and one day he said: "I know you're an intelligent man and an honest one. I would like to buy some wheat to sell in London, but I'm afraid of being accused of taking money from the King's treasures. Permit me to buy these goods in your name, and I will repay you." The man agreed.

As soon as they arrived in London, the captain suddenly passed away, and all his wheat continued belonging to the man. The wheat was worth much more than the original gem.

Rabbi Naḥman concluded by saying: "The precious stone was not meant to be his, and the proof of this is that it didn't go on being his. The wheat was destined to be his, and proof of this is that it was. *The reason for his success was that he knew how to control his nonsuccess.*" Nonsuccess is a momentary expression of *parnasah*, livelihood. The greater cycle—of *segulah*, treasure—remains unaltered. If we give this cycle time, it will recompose itself. In Yiddish we say: "A dash of luck is worth more than a pound of gold," or even "In the world of business, good *segulah* gets you further than correct decisions." *Segulah* is not luck, it's the combination of who we are and our importance to our own environment. We can make up for the absence of *segulah* using great effort, but those who enjoy this "treasure" realize that things come more easily to them. Of course, a good *segulah* is no guarantee of wealth; for that you have to be skilled in the art of interacting with the Market and transforming your *segulah* into wealth.

3

AMASSING WEALTH IN OTHER WORLDS

The Cycles of Wealth

The Kabbalah, when applied to money, deals with our exchanges with the Market. As we've seen, the Kabbalah refers not only to what we receive, but also to the balance between what we receive and what was available to us. This may sound like a massive rationalization, for we know from our day-to-day experience that those whom we consider to be wealthy are hardly ever worried about this balance. I won't try to prove that these people are not really rich. The rabbis, when approaching the theological problem of why the righteous suffer while the wicked prosper *(Tzaddik ve-ra lo, rasha ve-tov lo)*, avoid using logical systems to explain this phenomenon. The world in which we live is unfair, and however sad this may seem to us, there is no automatic debit mechanism where justice is concerned. It is so difficult to live with this fact that the Psalmist tells us:

> The fool cannot understand this:
> Though the wicked sprout like grass,
> though all evildoers blossom,
> it is only that they may be destroyed forever.
>
> *(Psalms 92:7-8)*

The rabbis, using a reincarnationist approach that exists in Jewish tradition, explain that there is always a return, that everything is revisited onto everybody by the law of retribution *(ḥok ha-gemul)*. Justice revisits wrongdoing from another dimension of time and reality. If galaxies have been transformed into human molecules and human molecules into galaxies, then everything must return, although the radius of the cycle is sometimes so large that to the naked eye of experience it seems like a straight line, running at a tangent.

These gigantic cycles of revisitation are analogous to the Buddhist concept of karma. Karmas are the costs and benefits of any Market. Today we identify them with ecological issues, where we are already beginning to hear the echoes of what formerly would never have reached us. In the past, the radius of the cycle was too large, but not anymore. The landowner who deforested his land seemed to enjoy all the benefits and none of the costs. Nowadays, these costs are so concrete that his descendants may even curse him, or the government may charge real fines, or he may even die of skin or lung cancer as a result of his misdeed. Even those who enjoyed the benefits when the radius seemed to tend to infinity paid their price in darkness. Let me explain what I mean by darkness. When we act in ignorance, we don't pay through the law of retribution, but through our very ignorance, our own darkness, which is in itself a price, a cost, and a shadow. When we act with knowledge, then we pay the costs as determined by the law of retribution.

This is not a dogma of faith that guarantees that the "wicked" will have to pay for their acts in the future. It is only a more sophisticated reading of what we observe in our daily experience.

Real wealth is a complex process, much more complex than the simple act of being in the right place at the right time. This is difficult to understand, but it is related to more elongated radii of cycles of return and to the four worlds of livelihood.

The Kabbalah speaks of four worlds to call our attention to the various dimensions of reality (see the table). This scheme helps us realize how biased we are: we tend to consciously recognize only those cycles of "receiving" that have very small radii of return.

In the world of Asiyyah (the functional world), we use logic to determine the benefits and the costs when the radius of the cycle is at its minimum. We worry about obtaining benefits as quickly as possible, and minimizing our costs in the short term. This is the mate-

World	Inner Dimension (Level of Perception)	Reality	Manifestation in Livelihood
ATZILUT Emanation	SOD Secret	CONNECTION TO THE INFINITE	LISHMAH ("For its own sake") Impossible to represent as gain
BERIAH Creation	DERASH Symbolic	SPIRITUAL	ZEKHUT Merit
YETZIRAH Formation	REMEZ Allusive	EMOTIONAL	SEGULAH Treasure
ASIYYAH Action	PESHAT Logical	MATERIAL	NEKHES Material Goods

rial world with all its complexities, as vast as the mind itself.

In the world of Yetzirah (emotional world), we have the inner treasure or, as we mentioned before, our potential for generating livelihood. This dimension is expressed as livelihood in both time and opportunity and is determined by the sum of our emotional history. The radius of the cycle is larger in this case, but still quite perceptible to the mind.

We often have this dimension in mind when we say of someone, "Everything he touches turns to gold."

In the world of Beriah (spiritual world), "merit" *(zekhut)* contributes to our livelihood as all the accumulated merit of the spiritual heritage passed down to us from our ancestors. *Zekhut* requires further definition.

Livelihood is a very complex concept. We can say, for example, that it's possible to make a living from writing books. Yet we can't eat, take shelter in, or medicate ourselves with books. The Market has made livelihood possible through education, through leisure, through service, and through so many other forms unknown in nature. Not even the symbiotic relationships in nature or the ecological exchanges between species come close to the human definition of Market. In nature there is only cooperation where vital livelihood is concerned; and in the Market, we find this at an emotional and spiritual level. So today, when we provide for ourselves, in some way we owe this possibility to an intricate and unrecoverable succession of "merits."

In the same way that I couldn't be eating and breathing today if my ancestors hadn't eaten or had sex, I can no longer tell whether I owe my existence to the apparently random influence of books that have been written, or to circuses that have been set up, or to the contribution of the postal service to society, for example. When someone spends his or her time writing a book, there is merit in this, just as there is in spending this same time changing diapers. In both cases, relationships are established with the Market, and these relationships make life feasible.

Our ancestors coded merits and introduced them

into the Market; and these merit-influences are like positive "karmas" that make life possible. There's a lot of power in this dimension, and we realize this when we evoke it.

In the central daily prayer of Judaism, when we consider ourselves to be face to face with the Divine, we ask, as a first introduction, to be identified as the descendants of the patriarchs and the matriarchs, because of their merits.* What they did in the past is, in some form (over very large cycles), coded into who we are and how we behave in the Market. These merits are the great pillar of our species, the foundation stone on which we base our livelihood and our rights (merits) as members of the Market. Because of its form, we only notice merit subjectively and collectively as cultural heritage. Understanding in what way our individual intentions and our own interference in the past (in past lives?) influences our livelihood and our concrete day-to-day life is a difficult matter. Our emotions grasp something of this reality, but only the spirit—unfettered as it is by the standards of our emotional and mental worlds—can access this dimension freely.

In the universe of Atzilut, for example, we would consider doing something just for the sake of doing it, with no expectation of gain. This world is concealed to us, open only to the undifferentiated, to that which is part of the One and part of Its very emanations.

*In the first blessing of the prayer, when we say, "Blessed are You, O God, our God and the God of our forefathers, God of Abraham, God of Isaac, and God of Jacob. . . ."

In the last dimensions, we have no organs of perception. Here we are fishing without a net—and when we do catch something, or believe that we do, it slips from our hands.

Can't or Won't?
Accepting the Incomprehensible

It is impossible to understand livelihood without understanding the intricate interrelationships inherent to life. Every "wealthy" person or anyone who is actively in search of livelihood can detect very subtle levels of exchange in the Market of life. This is why we worry so much about luck and at times feel that "something" is either on our side or working against us. Even those of us who are confined to more concrete dimensions of livelihood sense, in our day-to-day experience, the influence of strange forces.

A debate that took place just over two centuries ago may be useful as an example. It concerns the Baal Shem Tov, one of the most important figures of Jewish spiritual rebirth in the modern era. One day, he was sought out by a distinguished rabbi who wanted to question him about the intuitive and mystical elements that he stressed in his teachings. The stage was set for a classical encounter between two great tendencies. Human beings can be divided into those who see life as drenched in the very mystery that made it possible and those who, despite recognizing the mystery, don't see it as a constant agent in their day-to-day lives. The difference between human beings is not in how they see reality, but in the degrees of intensity of their similar beliefs. This difference distinguishes between rational-logical individuals and intuitive ones, between those who stress the chaotic elements of the universe and those who cultivate a more deterministic outlook—or even between those who express their beliefs in terms of Mystery or of God, and those who are less aware of the intervention of the inexplicable in their lives.

The Baal Shem Tov's meeting with this rabbi represents, in a very specific religious realm, the unending debate between these two tendencies. The description of this encounter, despite being in a language typical of Jewish tradition, has such universality that it could be translated to express this confrontation in any other tradition. At a certain moment, the discussion falls upon personal experiences and how we transform them into doctrine. The Baal Shem Tov tells a story from the Talmud (*Berakhot* 54b):

Rabbi Akiva was traveling with a donkey, a rooster, and a lamp one night, and he sought to spend the night at an inn in a village. The landlord refused to take him in, so Rabbi Akiva was forced to take shelter in a nearby wood, where he set up a small camp. During the night, his donkey was eaten by a lion. Rabbi Akiva wasn't in the least distressed. He thought to himself: "Maybe it is better this way." A little later, his rooster was attacked by a panther, and a strong wind blew out his lamp. Rabbi Akiva still remained calm: "Maybe it

is better this way." The following morning, when he returned to the village, he learned that it had been attacked during the night by a pack of bandits who had
ransacked the place and killed the inhabitants. He realized then that if his donkey and his rooster hadn't been
devoured and his lamp blown out, they would have be-
trayed his whereabouts. It had, in fact, been better that
way.

For the Baal Shem Tov this tale exemplified an
order that is only apparently the result of chaos or "bad
luck." Still not satisfied, the Baal Shem Tov insisted on
presenting his point of view through yet another example. He told the rabbi about one of his neighbors who
woke up one night because a mosquito had bitten him.
When the man got up, he realized that some embers
had fallen out of his fireplace onto the hearth, so he
fetched a bucket of water to put out what could have
led to a disaster. At that moment, the roof above his bed
fell in. If he had been asleep, he would have certainly
been crushed.

For the Baal Shem Tov these events and similar
experiences that we all go through point to intervention
beyond mere coincidence, free will, or instinct. But the
visiting rabbi saw the difficulties inherent to the examples cited by his opponent. Even further, the rabbi realized the immense danger involved in giving so much
credibility to the incomprehensible. His reaction was to
say: "I simply cannot believe that things are like that."

Once again, we face the logical stalemate that has
been going on for centuries. It might have remained yet

another frustrated attempt to bridge these two tendencies—but the Baal Shem Tov's reaction was impulsive: "It's not that you can't, but that you won't!" The rabbi didn't take these words seriously and left. He was riding back home through the forest, almost at dusk, when he saw a peasant whose cart had overturned trying to set it right. The peasant was desperate because he realized that he wouldn't be able to turn it over by himself, and so he waved to the rabbi asking for help. The rabbi, considering his age, the lateness of the hour, and the suddenness of the situation, answered immediately, "I'm sorry, but I can't." To which the peasant replied, "You can't or you won't?"

When the rabbi heard these words, he not only helped the peasant, but also returned to the Baal Shem Tov, to resume their conversation on a much different note. This same rabbi later became one of the Baal Shem Tov's greatest followers.

Our major difficulty when dealing with the incomprehensible, and with everything that belongs to the world of belief, is not that we can't accept things, but that we don't want to accept them. There is no language or reasoning that can explain the Baal Shem Tov's attitude. Only experience can show us that our problem is not "being able to," but "wanting to." We don't want to accept that our actions have consequences and reverberations that reach beyond our awareness and beyond our control. We don't want to see that our needs overreach what can be acquired, and that our convictions and beliefs could be mere illusions.

The Baal Shem Tov in his wisdom and vision understood that his best argument was time and experience, wherein the pieces of the puzzle would finally come together.

Livelihood and wealth are very important paths towards an awareness of these various dimensions of reality. Those who struggle for their livelihood know that there is something strange and miraculous in it. In the Market, in exchanges involving real money, we have many opportunities for discoveries and insights. The Baal Shem Tov knew that interactions in the Market are, in essence, exchanges with the world, and that they can teach what words and thoughts cannot. These interactions are the only way to unmask our supposed inability and reveal our true reluctance.

Owning versus Having

From this debate we draw a possible solution for a paradox that has bewildered us since primitive times: the evidence that there are righteous people who are burdened with lives of hardship and wicked people who are blessed with prosperity. What we must realize here is that disastrous or senseless realities can momentarily represent stages of a greater order.

It is fundamental, therefore, never to judge solely on the basis of a moment's snapshot of reality. Only in the midst of a dynamic reality can we truly take in and evaluate life's situations. This approach requires, most certainly, a large amount of faith and an understanding of these cycles of return that have longer radii.

There's an even more twisted way to read reality beyond simply registering the random injustice in our own daily experience. That is when we expect reality to follow the formula: "wicked people with bad (i.e., impoverished) lives and righteous people with good lives." To understand this better, let's carefully analyze the concepts of justice and merit. What are the situations in which we have the right to consider something as obtained righteously, through our own merit? How could Rabbi Akiva, in the story related above, be grateful for all the signs (or coincidences) that led him to feel protected by a greater force—Divine Providence (hashgaḥah)? How can a rich person comprehend his wealth as earned through merit? There is a terrible danger in all this.

Once, after I had completed a funeral service on a rainy day, the widow remarked, "Look, Rabbi, even God is crying." Her comment immediately found a counterpart in someone beside me who whispered: "Does that mean that when someone dies and the day is sunny, God is smiling?"

This same feeling is described by Elie Wiesel in reference to the survivors of the Nazi Holocaust. If people who were saved attribute their survival to God's intervention, saying, for example, that God watched over them, they will have to bear the responsibility of indirectly stating that God did *not* watch over all those who lost their lives. The relationships of causality that we establish have to account for all of reality in order to be considered answers. In other words, the Greek proposition whereby "luck is when the arrow hits someone else" expresses reality as seen from one individual's experience. The answers produced in this way are not careful to encompass all experiences. This is the ethical dimension of monotheism, where only one God, instead of my god or your god, must answer for all experiences using a single set of rules. A partial theological outlook deepens and reinforces the conviction that the righteous endure bad lives while the wicked enjoy good lives, as this in itself is also a partial proposition. Everything that doesn't take into consideration life as a whole will end up reinforcing our awareness of its unfairness. This kind of biased faith adds to the chaotic character of life. It turns against itself and becomes its own worst enemy when it encourages fragmentary perception and clouds our vision of the whole.

There's a paradox here. The more we see the world as the Baal Shem Tov advises us to—as a place where divine merit is ever-present—the less we can deny its chaotic nature. The poor must understand that they are poor because that is how things are, and not by mere coincidence. And the wealthy must perceive their wealth as the result of something beyond chance. At the same time, if we don't acknowledge this presence, we become overly materialistic and elevate chance and opportunity to the status of supreme masters of the Market. When we do this, we also add to the chaos of the universe.

To the naked eye of experience, on the surface, we can't break free of this paradox: the more faith we apply, the less faith we have. And faith, as we saw earlier, is an essential element of any Market. But the Baal Shem Tov was not referring to a faith that seeks, as an objective, to understand why the world is just or unjust. He was referring to a faith that seeks, in our deeper experiences, to understand the role of justice and injustice in the situations we go through. What is the meaning of each snapshot of reality, fair or unfair, in the development of our individual and collective paths?

This is the intuition that tells us when something is the result of "intervention" or when it's mere chance. The capacity to filter and lend authenticity to some phenomena and not to others is not pathological or irrational. It sprouts from the exact place where "heaven and earth kiss," where the soul touches the body.

This is what makes the widow see the rain as tears, while the survivor rejects his own experience as merely circumstantial.

The Baal Shem Tov himself reminds us that our "eyes" and "ears" must be trained to perceive a subtle reality around us. A *midrash* (*Genesis Rabbah* 10) urges us to recognize that every blade of grass has an angel standing over it, encouraging it: "Grow! Grow!" Until we grasp this dimension of order, while we refuse to dive deeper into the subtlety of each situation, we will continue to be caught up in the paradox and, hence, paralyzed. Our inferences must be checked using the insight of one who sees in the growth of the plants—

indeed, in everything—energies close at hand encouraging them to grow. If we observe life through these "eyes," then maybe the words *righteous* and *wicked, good* and *bad,* will take on a different meaning for us. The Market has certainly been formed, and is still being formed, in all its imperfections, under the profound influence of these eyes.

Questions such as "Why don't I have that?" or "Why do I have this?" demand answers that take into consideration the distribution of our potential across the various worlds of livelihood. Furthermore, "having" is not necessarily an absolutely positive value. "Having" can represent serious losses in other dimensions of livelihood. It can very often cancel out or erode our merits and "treasures." If we're not careful, we might use up too much of our personal and ancestral heritage in material form and pay a high price for this consumption.

Furthermore, owning something doesn't mean we effectively have it. And not owning doesn't necessarily mean we lack. Yet those who *really* own are blessed. I propose that we explore different manners of acquiring wealth in the various dimensions of livelihood that do not necessarily express themselves in the concrete world of Asiyyah.

4

MEASURING WEALTH
IN TERMS OF WHAT
WE DON'T HAVE

One of our greatest concerns in the business world is to avoid creating "anti-wealth." As we have learned, it is our duty, if we wish to "become rich," to increase the quality of life in the cosmos *(yishuv olam)*. If, however, in the process of transforming elements into abundance, we create some kind of scarcity, we are creating anti-wealth. We've seen that if we do this, we don't better the Market, and our behavior is considered anti-ecological and in opposition to the flow of life.

Anti-wealth introduced into the Market further corrupts it, increasing the overall levels of injustice. When we impoverish our worlds of treasure *(segulah)* or deplete our reserves of merit *(zekhut)*, we reduce the

Market's potential for order and wealth. And in doing this, we are going against the law of *yishuv olam* in a totally abstract and subtle dimension. The Rebbe of Kotzk exemplified this well:

Once, the Rebbe of Kotzk found himself on a road with a childhood friend of his who had become rich, but who had also become very careless in his duties as a wealthy man. Upon seeing the rabbi, the millionaire invited him into his splendid coach. Once inside the luxurious interior, the Rebbe took note of his affluence and asked, "Tell me . . . where are your possessions 'of this world'?"

The rich man replied, "Just look around you. Doesn't all that you see tell you something of my riches in this world?"

"No," answered the Rebbe, "they are your rewards taken from 'other worlds,' which you will lack in the world-to-come. What I would like to know is where your portion of wealth of *this* world is."

We often fail to pay attention to what account we are "withdrawing" from. And we fail to realize that the less we transform into material goods of our portion in other dimensions, the better. Only then will we possess the true measure of our livelihood, without using up our reserves from other worlds. One could even say that our true wealth is measured in terms of what we *don't* have. This statement is an extension of the ecological principle mentioned earlier: it is better to do nothing than to transform something into nothing. That is, it is wiser to leave riches in the form in which they have been bestowed to us. If, instead, we try to transform them into only one expression of wealth, we will find ourselves burdened with the double chore of materializing these riches into plenty in a single world of material livelihood, hence creating a scarcity of sustenance in other worlds and thus having to recover it later.

This internal ecology is essential. After all, how many times do we catch ourselves pushing forward along the path of material enrichment, later having to expend many of the same resources to remedy scarcity generated in other worlds of livelihood? We spend so much time and energy caught up in this cycle simply because we don't know how to mete out the proper amount of treasure and merit we wish to transform into ownership and power.

If this doesn't seem real to you, think of all the resources the Market must invest in order to deal with the depression, self-destructiveness, emotional poverty, boredom, and lack of meaning brought about by poor management of our resources in the different worlds. If we would only save up our emotional, spiritual, and transcendental energies, this Market would be in better shape, maybe even reaching the ideal conditions of the messianic age. The investment of our time resources in only a few forms of wealth has overly impoverished our Market, creating a kind of recession in higher worlds, where a large part of the population can't even guarantee minimal levels of exchange. This explains the lack of significant critical masses and healthy economies in this world. It's as if we were saturating the Market with emotional, spiritual, and transcendental insolvency. The term "third world," applied by economists to pockets of poverty and underdevelopment, is intuitively close to the mark. In Kabbalah, we would say that these masses are imprisoned in the "fourth world"—the material world of Asiyyah. Let us not forget, though, that poverty and underdevelopment belongs to all of us, no matter what social stratum we find ourselves in and of whether or not we consider ourselves materially wealthy.

The question that remains is: how can we avoid depleting resources in only one dimension of wealth? How can we create "customs" regulations for each of the various worlds until a messianic era may be installed, granting us a true "market economy" in these dimensions also?

Ideally, we should become rich without having more, and to attain this goal we must do battle on the toughest and most hostile terrain: everyday life.

Nonstealing

One of the most important ways in which we maximize resources in the different worlds of livelihood is through nonstealing.

We think that because we're not socially identified as thieves, stealing is far from our reality. Not so. Stealing is part of many of our interactions. And even small thefts affect the flow of riches within the Market. These small thefts reflect limitations in our personal and cultural background, more specifically our carelessness and our malice. I insist on calling them thefts to point out that, even though most of them are mental mechanisms, they are nonetheless deliberate actions that obstruct wealth in the Market.

The Bible (Leviticus 19:13)* classifies interactions related to theft into two groups: "withholding" *(osek)* and "misappropriation" *(gezel)*. Our social awareness singles out and punishes situations of misappropriation, but we rarely impose limits upon transactions that involve withholding. The difference between these two kinds of theft is defined by Maimonides. He states that *gezel* is the forceful appropriation of something that doesn't belong to us or that isn't available to us. By contrast, *osek* can be (a) the act of not returning something that has been taken, even with the owner's consent, or (b) the withholding of something that belongs to another, even if we don't mean to keep it. In committing these thefts, we interfere, act as obstacles, and keep things from being returned to their legitimate owners.

The first kind of *osek* described in the Talmud *(Bava Metzia* 111a) is when we constantly put off returning someone's belonging. The text exemplifies: "he comes and goes, comes and goes," and what is his is

*"Do not [unjustly] withhold that which is due your neighbor. Do not let a worker's wage remain with you overnight until morning" (Aryeh Kaplan translation).

53

not returned. This is unacknowledged theft and very similar to "misappropriation."

Examples of the second kind of *osek*, when we obstruct the owner's access to something, can be found in our daily lives. Let's look at some of the more common forms, such as theft of time, of expectation, and of information.

Theft of Time

Often we find ourselves in situations where, for reasons we don't entirely understand, we put off releasing information or making a decision. We postpone announcing decisions that we've already made and concerning which we don't intend to make any changes that would justify the delay. Why don't we immediately inform the other people concerned, possibly even admitting our ignorance, inability, or lack of interest? We postpone things for no reason at all and take up somebody's time. This is an enormous private tragedy for that person and his Market.

In most cases, this behavior is related to either carelessness or reluctance to face up to the circumstances. The consequences are not only the wasting of somebody's time, but the degeneration of this loss of time into embarrassing situations, conflict, and pain.

We are also guilty of *osek* when, to get rid of someone, we refer him to someone else who can supposedly help him, but who we know won't do that, for one reason or another.

All this goes against *yishuv olam,* enrichment of the world, and impoverishes the Market. So strong is the sensitivity of Jewish tradition to this kind of disrespect/theft that the following story is told about Rabbi Yishmael and Rabbi Shimon, who were being led to their execution during the persecution of Jews under the Roman emperor Hadrian:

Rabbi Shimon said to Rabbi Yishmael, "Master, my heart bleeds because I cannot find a reason for my execution."

Rabbi Yishmael answered, "Has it never happened that someone came to ask you for advice and you kept him waiting until you finished what you were drinking, or until you finished tying your shoes or changing your clothes? The Torah says: 'and if you should come to withhold *[osek].* . . .' This refers to trivial cases as well as to serious ones."

Rabbi Shimon sighed and said, "You have comforted me, my Master."

In this very dramatic way, the rabbis equated disrespect for another's time with an assault on life. If we steal property, we are punished by the justice system, but when we steal time, we easily get away with it. According to Jewish tradition, the dimensions of space and time both belong to God. If we spend the lifespan divinely accorded to us in wasting our neighbor's time, we are robbing the Market of all the possible "wealth" that could have been generated using this time. We are responsible for the costs that the Market incurs while absorbing this deficit in potential.

Theft of Expectation

Another example the rabbis drew from *osek* is that of the worker and his wage. The Bible says: "On the same day that he finishes his work, pay his wage; the sun should not set with him waiting for it—because his life depends on it (Deuteronomy 24:15). Here we are not even considering any depreciation that the salary might suffer as a result of the delay, because that would be *gezel* (misappropriation). This case refers exclusively to workers' expectations of receiving what is due them to use in any way they see fit.

If we withhold someone's wages, it is as if we were robbing him of his expectation of having the money at the exact moment that it comes to belong to him. Even if we later return the same value, we are depriving the owner of his right.

The same applies to false expectations we may give salespersons. If we demonstrate false interest, allowing them to count on a possible entrance of capital, we are also stealing expectations. Whether we act motivated only by a wish to be "nice" or by a deliberate desire to generate expectations, we must realize the potentially serious implications of this behavior. This is because "expectations" are an indication that we are treading on extremely delicate terrain—that of human relationships. We should always try to be aware of the boundary between personal experiences and transactions that establish interactive ties.

This is one of the important elements of theft:

withholding *(osek)* can only occur in situations where interaction and transaction occur. The rabbis warn us to be very sensitive and conscientious when entering transactions, because in this dimension we are no longer completely independent: we must take into consideration our partner and his or her reality. A transaction is safely within the Market if our gain is maximum in relation to the maximum gain of the other while generating minimum waste or disturbance of the universe. Thus, when we take a step towards a transaction, we must be very careful indeed.

Another common kind of theft of expectation is gambling. Anyone who plays the lottery expects to win. If the gambler is not very clear about the minimal chances of fulfilling this expectation, then the lottery could be considered a kind of theft. This is because gamblers enter the transaction with the expectation of leaving it with something, only to discover later on that their chances were less than zero right from the start.

Theft of Information

Another form of withholding *(osek)* is holding back information that would permit *yishuv olam*, a greater wealth of the universe. Many times we are called upon to advise others, and this form of transaction can also lead to theft.

If someone asks you for directions to a certain address, you can simply say, 'Turn left at the corner and go five blocks." If, however, you know of any important information, you should share it. We find the following commentary in *Sifra,* a legal commentary on the Book of Leviticus: "If someone comes seeking your counsel, don't advise him incorrectly. Don't say, for example, "Go early," when you know that bandits can attack him; or "Go at noon," when you know the sun is unbearable.

When we give information, we should ask ourselves deep inside how we would advise ourselves. In this we rely on the principle that the Bible uses for all questions of theft through oppression: "Love your neighbor as yourself" (Leviticus 19:18). Herein lies a great clue to enriching the Market. If someone asks us how to get somewhere, we should advise her in such a way that she not only reaches her destination, but reaches it safely and quickly. How many times, out of sheer laziness or lack of consideration, do we share only fragments of our knowledge?

It is our duty to share knowledge, provided that we don't lose anything as a result of this sharing and someone else gains. We established this principle when we talked about the "law of neighbors," which states that "one person gains and the other loses nothing." The losses resulting from withholding information can be high-priced, both financially and physically (owing to the dangers incurred), or even emotionally and spiritually. If we don't identify situations of possible spiritual and emotional erosion, we are responsible for this omission. We could be contributing to the impoverishment

THE KABBALAH OF MONEY

of various worlds—and the deficits will be our responsibility.

A Stumbling Block before the Blind

From the well-known biblical saying (Leviticus 19:14) "Do not put a stumbling block before the blind" *(lifnei iver)* the rabbis draw an important concept: it is our duty to pay attention not only to the interactions we engage in, but also to the people we deal with in these interactions. With this in mind, let's expand a little on this "visual" notion of going through life placing stumbling blocks before the blind.

To begin with, who is "blind"? All those whose "vision" is less than ours. We ourselves are also blind in relation to certain other people, and in those cases the responsibility is theirs when interacting with us. Whoever sees farther owes this responsibility to the Market. A few examples will help to clarify this.

If we leave money lying around on a table in front of a very needy person, or even someone who has previously given in to the impulse to "misappropriate" something, we are placing a stumbling block before the blind. A person in need, or someone who has bad habits, is blind in this interaction, and our carelessness is a stumbling block for him or her.

For the rabbis, the jeweler who leaves precious gems out on a table to be stolen by an employee also shares in the cost of this theft in other worlds. Not only does he lose his property, but he himself is declared a thief: he has robbed himself of the opportunity of saving a "blind" person from stumbling. On a similar basis, Maimonides prohibits the sale of armaments to thieves or warring peoples.

The Talmud gives more examples of people guilty of placing a stumbling block before the blind:

- A father who physically attacks his grown son possibly causes him to "blindly" retaliate and do something reprehensible (*Moed Katan* 17a).
- A person who serves as a scribe for an illegal transaction is an accomplice to the crime. His stumbling block is to permit the "blind" to go through with their transaction (*Bava Metzia* 75b).
- Someone who lends money without witnesses or a contract violates the prohibition against putting a stumbling block before the blind (*Bava Metzia* 75a).

So we see that our carelessness can not only cause monetary losses to ourselves, but also induce others to commit crimes that will cost them dearly. As long as this world remains unredeemed, it is important to draw up contracts very carefully, with close attention to every detail—not because we are suspicious or miserly, but in order to restrain the bad impulses that are present in all human beings. A Yiddish saying warns us: "If you don't think about the law, you'll end up involved with it."

Contracts are a very important issue in transactions. Good contracts are essential to the improvement of the Market. And every badly drawn-up contract in life generates disastrous costs in the form of anti-wealth, theft, loss of time, and conflict. Moreover, such contracts have great influence in the higher worlds of livelihood, where they impoverish our treasures and merits.

Theft of Reputation

From another biblical text—"Do not go around as a gossiper among your people" (Leviticus 19:16)—the rabbis also identify a kind of theft. We often damage the Market with the information we spread.

We are referring here not to slander *(motzi shem ra)*, as this would be "misappropriation," not "withholding." We are talking about the spreading of true information that may be uncomplimentary *(lashon hara,* "evil tongue"). Maimonides comments on this:

> One who speaks ungenerously of another is one who sits and says: "This is what he did, this is what his parents did, and this is what I heard about him. . . ." This may be what the Psalmist had in mind when he said: "May the Lord cut off all the lips that do not rest and the tongue that speaks proudly" (Psalms 12:3).
>
> Our sages say that to speak maliciously of others is the worst of crimes and equivalent to forsaking God. An evil tongue hurts three people:

the one who speaks, the one who is spoken of,
and the one who listens—the one who listens
more than the one who speaks.

The big problem of the evil tongue is that it belit-
tles indiscriminately. The person who listens to the
rumor doesn't know the limits of the reality insinuated
through the facts that he's told. The very tone of voice
used can cause great unnecessary damage in the many
worlds of livelihood.

A concrete example is the case of a small creditor
who, though aware of the scope of his act, demands the
foreclosure of a company. In response to rumors, the
other creditors, especially the larger ones, also file for
foreclosure. The company loses its credibility and has
to shut down. The small creditor's attitude may have
robbed the company of its possibility of recovering. In
exchange for the amount owed to him, this creditor
takes on the responsibility for hundreds of workers
being laid off and many years of work going down the
drain, and he incurs the anger and resentment of many
people. These costs in other worlds are merely repara-
tions he must pay to compensate for his theft of reputation.

Speech, then, is a transaction, in which decisions
are made and fates are decided—and the responsibility
for careless or malicious speech is shouldered by whoever spreads the information and whoever listens to it.

This kind of talk pollutes the environment and destroys the Market. Its potential for destruction is so

great that it is classified under the commandment "Do not prostitute the earth" (derived from Leviticus 19:29). The evil tongue can be compared to nuclear weapons: its destructive force spreads in a powerful chain reaction and remains in the air for a long time, slowly killing off the possibilities of a healthy Market.

Tzedakah: The Antidote to Theft

The English word *charity* is used to translate the Jewish concept of *tzedakah*. The nature of tzedakah, however, is not related to the literal meaning of charity, which comes from the Latin *caritas*, "love." The Jewish meaning is associated with the Market and should be translated literally as "justice" *(tzedek)* or, if I may be permitted a neologism, the act of "justicing."

Tzedakah is a key issue in Jewish tradition. Whereas Christianity stresses love as uppermost in establishing a messianic era, Judaism emphasizes justice. When we love our neighbor, we do so through discerning what is fair. According to Judaism, if people understood that all interactions are taxed proportionally to our various levels of interdependence, the messianic era would be a reality.

This co-responsibility that we all share demands that our day-to-day life be filled with "justice adjustments," tzedakah. In the same way that love is not only tenderness, but also recognizing your partner's needs, tzedakah is not only the meting out of justice, but a giving of oneself on all levels: from individual to individual, to other species, and to the environment.

Tzedakah is of fantastic importance to the Market. It is one of its intelligent operators, translating our attitudes into a desire for "enrichment of the cosmos." And it is a fundamental tool in preventing waste. A Hasidic commentary says: "When the load on the back of a camel tilts and begins to fall, only one man is needed to put it back in place. But if the entire load falls to the ground, not even four or five men can pick it up and replace it. It's the same with tzedakah: a little today will accomplish what a lot tomorrow may not be able to do."

Judaism says that all kinds of wealth are interconnected. And if wealth doesn't seek to ameliorate poverty, then by definition, it impoverishes itself. There can be no neutrality in poverty. In this universe, there are either ascending or descending riches. We'll see this in detail further on. First, let me point out two types of impoverishment that come about when we ignore tzedakah.

One, there are *subtle* interconnections that can generate impoverishment. The Rabbi of Chelm—the city of the dull-witted, whose inhabitants, in their own peculiar way, end up by expressing much wisdom—reproached a certain wealthy man for being "irresponsible" towards the poor. He said: "We read in Deuteronomy [15:11]: *The poor will never cease to exist upon the face of the earth.* From this we can conclude that if you let the poor die of hunger, some of you will have to

become poor to take their place and justify the words of
God." The rabbi is trying to establish that there is a
network of communicating vessels between the various
kinds of wealth. And he goes on to say, cleverly trying
to enlist the wealthy men's cooperation, that it is necessary for the maintenance of their own wealth that they
take responsibility for the poor.

Two, there are *concrete* interconnections that can
generate impoverishment. The Rabbi of Mezibuzh commented on the verse *The righteous man will eat until
he satisfies his appetite; but the wicked will still hunger*
(Proverbs 13:25): "This refers to a guest who comes to
the home of a righteous or a wicked person. The righteous person invites the guest to eat, and he eats also,
even if he has already done so, so as not to embarrass
his guest. The wicked man, by contrast, even if he is
hungry, endures the hunger pangs instead of partaking
of the meal with his guest."

Much existing wealth cannot be made available to
us, because of our unwillingness to share. And this unwillingness generates situations that range from embar-
rassment to violence, and ends up by depriving the
wealthy of a better life because they avoid their allotted
responsibilities. They will end up by sharing the banquet, but not enjoying it. The righteous, on the other
hand, even if they're already satisfied, will take pleasure in the simple act of sharing.

We could say, based on the principle "Do not put
a stumbling block before the blind," that those who do
not fulfill their responsibilities of tzedakah are increas-

ing the number of "blind" people in the world. If there are more "blind" people in the world, many more situations will become obstacles and there will be much less freedom. Wealth without tzedakah impoverishes the Market and reduces its levels of freedom.

Tzedakah is yet another example of "how to become rich while having less."

The Technique of Tzedakah

Tzedakah is not only a concept, it's also a practice and a technique. As an art, it cannot be practiced in a literal fashion. That is, tzedakah doesn't mean mechanically setting aside a percentage of your profit for donations at the end of the fiscal year. It demands, above all, involvement, creativity, and wisdom.

The dynamics of tzedakah are linked to *gratitude*, which can be defined as a measure of our capacity to withdraw from the riches of other worlds. Gratitude is an expression of how interconnected the riches of the different worlds are for an individual, so that no matter how poor someone may seem in one world, there are always riches to be transferred from the account of another world. In that sense we can see gratitude as a path that, passing through ecology and well-being, leads to livelihood. When we realize the deep levels of happiness that we draw from health, opportunities, and exchanges, we tend to push ourselves constantly towards tzedakah.

Tzedakah should be an everyday practice, performed with grace and wisdom. It should be one of the most desirable goods for sale at the huge supermarket of existence. There are few pleasures that match that of tzedakah when it is well performed—namely, when it is the product of spontaneity and sincerity as opposed to social demand. Those who practice and apply tzedakah will find themselves drawn to involuntary acts that are a great source of joy and surprise. These acts reveal an inner self that becomes better, richer, and more capable of enjoying the various worlds.

But what would we consider everyday tzedakah?

Try to measure, by tuning in to your livelihood, how much gratitude each personal gain affords you. This gratitude is the measure you should use to tax your gains. And the more accurately taxed these gains are, the more life they will provide.

If you are blessed with gains that exceed your expectations, and your efforts were surprisingly low, you should take pleasure in taxing this profit with plenty of tzedakah.

When you lose an object and find it again, tzedakah is also called for. For a few moments you no longer possess that belonging and you realize how ephemeral ownership is. When this object returns to you, try making a movement towards tzedakah, donating part of your gain. When we lose something, we understand not only the cost of things but also the implicit value of ownership. This is the gratitude that I speak of: becoming aware of the value that something or somebody has for us.

When we lose our health and later recover it, there should also be some tzedakah involved. Of course, we don't need to lose something to be grateful for what we have. In fact, the true essence of tzedakah is to be able to tax ourselves more accurately when we're well and in good health. But we know that it's part of the learning process towards being a constant performer of tzedakah, to test our training in situations that speak of our true possessions, their vulnerability, and the gift they represent.

Taking advantage of the tzedakah opportunities that life offers is an art accessible only to those who are more sensitive to life's mechanisms. Tzedakah is to be seen as a genuine opportunity, as in the following story.

The Ropshitzer Rabbi's wife said to her husband, "Your sermon was long today. I wonder how it was received and whether the rich will be more generous in their contributions to the poor."

The rabbi answered, "Half of my audience was pleased. The poor have agreed to accept the contributions!"

For the Rabbi of Ropshitz, the very opportunity for tzedakah is a blessing. According to him, someone who is really wealthy and knows how to enjoy all the Market possibilities is grateful even for the opportunity of being an agent of tzedakah.

From this we conclude that it is a great gift and advantage to have the opportunity to perform tzedakah.

When we realize this, it's a sign that we have broken through one of the limitations *(kelippot)* that keep us from enjoying the best of the worlds of livelihood.

Tzedakah Therapy

There are times when a rabbi will look into somebody's eyes and, like a doctor or psychotherapist, he will diagnose a deficiency of tzedakah. With this ailment comes a lowered resistance to loss, a corrosion of our communication lines with the world, and the worst kind of sickness: poor self-knowledge.

The phenomenon of well-being and happiness can be deconstructed into minimal structures (quantum-happiness) that sprout from our capacity to keep "up-to-date" with ourselves. The more we know and understand ourselves, the easier it is for us to find our way in life. Much in the same way that someone who has her debts under control and knows her financial obligations in the near future sleeps easily, one who knows herself reasonably well awakens easily.

However incredible this may seem, not being up-to-date with our tzedakah is one of the problems that drains our vitality most. After all, tzedakah is one of the few elements we can dispose of to produce meaning and detachment in our lives. And too much attachment, or a life led as if it were a poker game, where we don't share with our partners, is a source of great tension and distress. If we look closely, the way we deal with tzedakah can be revealing of tendencies, symptoms, and deviations. And this is where tzedakah can be both diagnostic and therapeutic at the same time: it's a Kabbalistic X-ray of the current "state of exchange," revealing life's magic at a given instant.

If we see tzedakah as a tool for self-knowledge, we learn to cherish it. It becomes a new parameter, a measure of who we are. And who we are in tzedakah is exactly who we are in reality. When we begin to understand the true meaning of tzedakah, we learn to sense and honor our own limitations.

How difficult it is to give! I don't mean giving in situations where the radius of the cycle of return is small, but giving when there is apparently no kind of recompense. It is not the "giving" that we find an excuse to do in public in order to earn approval, respect, or deference, but the painful giving to which there is no witness but ourselves. In this giving, we value our individuality enough to be true to ourselves and our deepest instincts.

It is important to reflect upon tzedakah, make it more real, and not allow it to degenerate into a paternalistic relationship towards the world. A paternalistic attitude makes for easy disregard of tzedakah as a mere remnant of an unsophisticated past when people knew little about themselves. Our attitude should be the exact opposite, for tzedakah is a precious legacy produced by the sensitivity of those who understood life in all its depths. If you are still having trouble comprehending the importance of tzedakah kabbalistically, you can try a "hierarchy" exercise on the distinct powers of this world, as Rabbi Yehudah did:

> Stone is hard, but iron cuts it. Iron is stiff, but fire melts it. Fire is powerful, but water extinguishes it. Water is heavy, but clouds carry it. Clouds are strong, but wind disperses them. Wind is strong, but the body resists it. The body is strong, but fear destroys it. Fear is strong, but wine averts it. Wine is strong, but sleep conquers it. Death is more powerful than any of these, but tzedakah redeems death. *(Midrash Tanḥuma)*

The statement "Tzedakah redeems death" can be understood as referring either to actual death or to the fear and anguish associated with death. Rabbi Yehudah makes careful analogies so that we don't take his words literally. If we look closely, we'll see that the measures of "strong" and "powerful" refer to human beings. His sequence takes a human outlook on "power." It's through our human perception that we are encouraged to analyze it. And this sequence is purposefully designed by Rabbi Yehudah so as to increase in strength as it decreases in concreteness, towards more abstract and conceptual examples.

First, he mentions the more concrete elements of our human imagery of strength—stone and iron. Next, we go to more abstract but still concrete elements—clouds and wind. From this point onwards, Rabbi Yehudah dives into the body and uncovers a doorway into an inner world, where strength is related to our ability to cope with life in the face of our fears. The next link of the chain tells us how to overcome fear through something more powerful: pleasure. Wine and sleep can control fear when we're in a position to enjoy them—when we're healthy. The importance and the great power of human beings emerge from the difficulties we go through in trying to cope with life, not only at a given moment, but in its deeper questions of anguish and loneliness. The word used by Rabbi Yehudah is "death," the anguish of death. Overcoming it is only possible through a more abstract power, more conceptual than death itself. This power is tzedakah. Sublime, and deeply imbedded in the soul, it's the height of human sophistication—our most powerful tool.

To a certain degree, what Rabbi Yehudah is telling us is that beyond "death," beyond the concept of death, lies the concept of life, of meaning, and of exchange. We must be careful, however, when we use a technical word like *tzedakah* in contrast to another, not less technical term: the word *death* as employed by Rabbi Yehudah. Death is an abstraction (though at times it seems all too concrete) of nonexchange, just as tzedakah is a concrete abstraction of exchange.

Whoever understands this and sets aside time for tzedakah is a master of life. He goes beyond his limitations, dispels anguish, and receives therapy. It is the kind of therapy we must constantly undergo in order to bring us from who we were a moment ago to who we are now—a necessary transformation that is impossible if

we exclude the elements of the pocket and a balance in
the dimension of tzedakah.

Tzedakah as Business

When we truly understand the value of tzedakah, we
recognize it as a kind of wealth. It can be accumulated
and negotiated, and should be pursued with the same
zeal that we devote to any commercial transaction that
interests us.

If this seems difficult, let me draw your attention
to two rabbinical examples. The first implies that tzedakah is governed by laws similar to those of any other
negotiations—and that, in a very indirect, almost im-
perceptible way, tzedakah is a means of livelihood for
the person who practices it. The laws of the Market and
the care we devote to our businesses should be applied
also to our tzedakah. This is what Reb Shmelke shows
us in the following story.

Once, Reb Shmelke found himself with no money
in his pocket to give to a beggar. So he went to his wife's
drawer, took out a ring, and gave it to the man. When
his wife came home and discovered that the ring was
gone, she began to cry. When Reb Shmelke explained
what had happened, she demanded that he run after the
pauper, as the ring was worth over fifty talents.

Running desperately, the rabbi managed to catch
up with the beggar. He grabbed the man and said: "I've
just discovered that the ring I gave you is worth more

than fifty talents. Don't let anyone trick you into accepting less!"

The story holds us in a material dimension until the very end, when we realize that Reb Shmelke lived in another dimension of the world of money altogether. In this dimension, he could only interpret his wife's concern as a desire that the poor man not be tricked regarding the value of her tzedakah. This may seem like a surprise ending, but if you read it equipped with an understanding of the world of livelihood, everything makes sense from beginning to end.

Another example is that of Reb Eliezer, who, based on his comprehension of livelihood, tracked down tzedakah opportunities like a greedy businessman.

The charity collectors were in the habit of hiding from Reb Eliezer, because he would often give all he had to charity. Once he went to the market to buy a wedding dress for his daughter, and when the charity collectors saw him coming, they tried to run away. But he saw them first and followed them. When he found them, he begged, "Tell me, what do you have today for tzedakah? What cause are you collecting for?" They answered, "We're collecting funds to buy a wedding dress for a poor girl who is about to get married." Reb Eliezer thought to himself, "This girl takes priority over my daughter," and he donated all he had, keeping only a zuz. With this zuz he bought a handful of wheat, which he placed in a room in his house.

When his wife came home, she asked her daughter, "What has your father brought for you?" And the daughter answered: "Whatever it is, it's over there in that room." The mother went to the room and couldn't open the door, because there was wheat piled high up to the ceiling.

When he arrived home, Reb Eliezer was approached by his wife, who said, "Come see what the Creator has done for you." When Reb Eliezer saw what had happened, he said, "This wheat must be distributed among the poor, and we must only keep a portion equivalent to that of those people who don't have money to buy a wedding dress for their daughters."

The main element of this story is not the miraculous reward, but the constantly coherent attitude of Reb Eliezer: coherent, that is, for someone who understands reality in a specific way. In the beginning, we see that the charity collectors hide from him as if they were the very source of his business and livelihood. And that is exactly how Reb Eliezer sees them—as opportunities for livelihood. His very wording when he finds them has us believing that he's really shopping around the Market for opportunities: "What do you have today for tzedakah?" Even the story's setting, the market, is suggestive of the scope of this Market and its possibilities. After all, how many of us walk around shopping for opportunities as Reb Eliezer does?

Even the apparently dogmatic ending, where he keeps only the equivalent of the dress, is just another demonstration that he inhabits a parallel universe. Reb Eliezer goes to the market to buy a wedding dress for his daughter, and he leaves this Market with a dress:

not with a material dress, but with his money completely distilled. It is now a responsible money that can
finally buy a real dress. But we may ask: Didn't Reb
Eliezer have the money already? And who said the
money was clean? Reb Eliezer said so. Reb Eliezer realized that to buy a dress for his daughter when others
could not implicated him in some way. Above all, he is
not passive, and he's not a fool who throws his money
away, as it may seem at first sight. He holds on to his
zuz, which is the financial link between the nonrespon-
sible money and the money that has been taxed with
responsibility.

And if you're still wondering whether, if you try
this out, your wheat will be multiplied too, remember:
Reb Eliezer's attitude as a human being is more incredible and miraculous than the actual multiplication of
the wheat. Maybe our story uses this symbol of "multiplied wheat" to point out the unbelievable possibilities
that would open up to us if we disarmed and walked
through the Market with Reb Eliezer's voracity. Of
course, we must remember that voracity doesn't mean
producing just any kind of transaction with our capital
but, rather, *responsible* transactions.

These are unquestionable demonstrations of
wealth derived from having—temporarily and apparently—less. They are outlooks on livelihood where the
radius of the cycle of return is large—ecological, even.

5

WEALTH INCREASED BY
HAVING LESS

Ecology and Justice

The rabbis understand ecology as being part of the dimension of tzedakah. It isn't charity, but an investment in justice. Let's try to think of these two words together: justice and ecology. What is just? Better still, how can Reb Eliezer know that a wedding dress for a poor girl takes precedence over his daughter's dress? If his behavior were the result of sentimentality, or morality, or the decision of a shlemiel (a simpleton), Reb Eliezer would be ravishing the Market. It is therefore of extreme importance for the preservation of his capital that Reb Eliezer know what is just. If his choice is not just, if it's not the appropriate measure, he will further confuse the Market. He simply becomes a poor man incapable of giving his daughter a wedding dress, hence imposing upon the collectors two tasks: providing a dress for a poor girl and another one for Reb Eliezer's daughter. This destroys the Market through the foolish premise that "what is mine is yours and what is yours is mine."

The *Mishnah* (oral code of laws) alludes to the meaning of property and justice by exemplifying four types of attitudes:

> Those who say, "What is mine is mine and what is yours is yours," are like the inhabitants of Sodom and Gomorrah.
> Those who say, "What is mine is yours and what is yours is mine too," are foolish.
> Those who say, "What is mine is yours and what is yours is yours too," are righteous.
> And those who say, "What is mine is mine and what is yours is mine too," are wicked.

Let's decode what is being said here. "What is mine is yours and what is yours is mine" and "What is mine is mine and what is yours is mine too" are clearly the behavior of the foolish and the wicked. The first is similar to the proposition whereby "it is better to do nothing than to transform something into nothing," and the second is a typical case of unmitigated greed. The other two attitudes require more thought, because it is between these two wavelengths that our human tendencies oscillate.

The stance that would seem neutral ("What is mine is mine and what is yours is yours") is said to be similar to the behavior of the corrupt communities of Sodom and Gomorrah. This idea derives from the rabbinical premise that we cannot detach ourselves from our community, for life happens within relationships and among people or, as we've nowadays come to believe, within our interactions with all living things, including plants and animals. Isolation is an illusion that is responsible for much individual and collective instability. The pragmatism of "What is mine is mine and what is yours is yours" is a great ecological threat, because it tends to create societies or life networks that are cancerous and self-destructive. For the rabbis, the "Sodom and Gomorrah" philosophy is symbolic of something that drifts ever so imperceptibly from its path and eventually brings about its own extinction. Thus God programs His creation, leaving in it the self-destructive software necessary to stop it from going against its basic commands. The interdependence of livelihood and survival is a lot broader than simply, "What is mine is mine and what is yours is yours." It's an ecological network that encompasses orbits of return of various different magnitudes.

The behavior of the righteous also seems foolish if we consider that, righteous or not, they must survive and make a living. If it's true that "what is mine is yours and what is yours is yours too," then the righteous will soon starve and freeze. The *Mishnah* does not aim to ignore the more immediate orbits of return as part of life. That would be absurd. It wishes only to enhance our awareness of *hospitality*—the understanding that we are guests of God. We are guests in an immense and intricate web where the most sophisticated form of consciousness lives by the rule "What is mine is not mine and what is yours is yours."

Paradoxical and unjust as this may seem, "What is mine is not mine" shows a willingness to partake of all the riches of these worlds without clinging to the poverty of what is offered us in small cycles of return. And "What is yours is yours" is a prerequisite for any kind of recompense.

It is as if we were talking about efforts in opposite directions that complement each other. Individually, we should progress towards detaching ourselves from the idea of property in its more concrete and material form. And when dealing with others, we should progress towards recognizing, unconditionally, the right of ownership in its most down-to-earth, concrete form. When we reach these objectives, we are truly rich.

The ecologist, like the good guest, rids himself of the weight and of the limits of "having" by saying that "what is mine is yours and what is yours is yours too." In having less, he really has more.

Even if all this makes sense and we are content with it, we mustn't forget that understanding is only an infinitesimal step towards transforming ourselves into what we understand. Once more, we come to the question: How can we be fair? Is not fairness the sum of all situations, causes, and things involved in the immediate, medium, and long term? If so, it's impossible to be absolutely fair. Once we understand this, we need no longer be paralyzed. We can be sure of the great responsibility we share for what we see through the light of our conscience. And no matter how blind we are to the whole, we are not released from the responsibility of being discerning. In other words, justice, for us human beings, is becoming progressively more complex. And that's good. This world is, for conscientious human beings, a world of ever more intricate systems of livelihood. Our family feeling is larger and wider; and our perception of hospitality is also sharper.

There's a rule in hospitality: the more a guest respects his host, the greater the pleasure the host derives from offering his home, even lavishing on his guest more attention than what he would normally offer. The less respect there is, the shorter will be the stay.

A good guest is an example of owning less (not even what is yours is truly yours) and thus having more.

Learning and Ecology

In the first chapter we saw that learning or study is considered, in Jewish tradition, to be the only antidote to wasted time. Collectively, our studies are an ecological manifestation. Professor Ismar Schorsch, Chancellor of the Jewish Theological Seminary in New York, explains in a brilliant article entitled "Learning to Live with Less" that the objective of study is to determine not what people should do with their time, but what they should do with their *free* time. According to him, "Tradition invites us to cultivate inner life in such a way that it counterbalances the tensions and seductions of prosperity and oppression." Free time that fails to generate real livelihood, that isn't used affectionately towards our neighbor or for leisure, multiplies our needs and accumulates riches of other worlds in this dimension.

Consumerism is a great source of our ecological problems. We're tricked into thinking that we need to own more in order to have more. This search for a balance in the different worlds, and not only in the concrete and material world, is directly related to studying. For the rabbis, "studying" is a very specific livelihood terminology that means investment and enrichment in other worlds. Knowing how to study is ecological; it means knowing how to extract from our consciousness, which constantly seeks to dominate and conquer (thus keeping us trapped in the material Market), the pathways that lead to higher dimensions of livelihood.

Presents and Tips

> One who gives cools the fire of ambition for wealth.
> —*Yiddish saying*

What we've seen so far about wealth being increased by having less is that avoiding the obsession with getting rich is also a kind of real wealth. It's not only that this

---

obsession makes our access to wealth more difficult, but that, as the Talmud says, "One who seeks treasures hastens the day of his death."

We should be constantly monitoring our levels of ambition. I noted earlier that tzedakah and study are in themselves forms of wealth and options that are open to us when we are trying to transform "less" into "more." And we can extend this concept to relationships that are milder, though not less day-to-day, such as those involving presents and tips.

Presents and tips are important antidotes to the obsession with wealth: they cool the fire of ambition. Have you ever had the great pleasure of giving a gift whose cost would have been enough to buy yourself anything you wanted? Yet nothing could surpass the feeling experienced through this kind of giving. The same applies to a good tip. How many times have we hesitated before paying a bill, or before repaying someone who has been of inestimable use to us, and confronted the dilemma, "Should I leave with more in my pocket or leave the change on the table?" How many times have we experienced in the tip artistically applied a feeling of having given our money a value that we could never have obtained by buying something? This gives us an idea of what a good investment tips and presents can be.

When we face the dilemma "to give or not to give," it is because we've reached the limits of our pocket. And it's in the pocket that tzedakah, time allotted to study, gifts, and tips are all decided.

Less Is More

Pockets are quadrangular in shape, dark, constantly in-
vaded and penetrated, and they bring forth decisions
that translate into life or death. The moment of the
pocket is the frontier of a transaction, when we really
demonstrate how we see the world—and how much of
it we see. With a hand deep in our pocket, we're alone,
face to face with our self; it is a moment comparable
only to the instant where we face the open refrigerator
on a diet. *Who are you?* The answer will come from your
pocket.

Our rationalizations, our self-image, the images we
project onto others—all of this is challenged by the
pocket. The pocket unmasks us to others and ourselves,
revealing where we are and how much we see.

Let us stretch our imagination a little further by
considering the following situations.

Situation 1 (tzedakah): You are in your car waiting
at a traffic light, lost in thought, when you realize that a
beggar is approaching you. His words mouthed at your
window transport you to the realm of the pocket and put
you on the spot. Certain questions occur to you: to give
or not to give, to help or not to help; shame; invasion of
privacy; fear of being tricked; guilt; empathy; fantasies
that you are the beggar; the possibility of being saved
from the situation in a few seconds when the light
changes to green; the sensation of being stuck there
forever. Your heart becomes your pocket and your
pocket must answer for you. You *are* your pocket, and it

THE KABBALAH OF MONEY

must pronounce the verdict. Nothing is neutral any longer, because you're "in a transaction." Now you inevitably fall into one of the four attitudes that the *Mishnah* suggests as possible ways to respond to a transaction, as described at the beginning of this chapter: you are either *"nothing," foolish, righteous,* or *wicked.*

Situation 2 (present): You have the opportunity to give a gift, a spontaneous present that involves no return or payment. It would be a present expressing affection beyond any duty. You have the gift in front of you. It's beautiful, it's perfect for the person; but it's expensive. In your heart you know that giving this gift would be great, but not giving it would not harm the relationship either. You think to yourself: What is money? Money is a lot, and what if I'm going too far? What if I could show the same affection with something more symbolic? But how can you deny yourself the pleasure of this gift if you've already imagined it to be perfect? You can only come out of this situation as a nothing, a fool, one who sees, or one who doesn't see. The gap between buying the present or not is small, and it depends upon an impulse from the heart to the pocket—and this is the longest of paths.

Situation 3 (tip): You've just received news that someone has created an opportunity for you that promises considerable extra profit. Your first impulse is one of total gratitude, and you think of compensating him accordingly. After some time has passed, however, and you place your earnings in perspective, up against your endless needs, all your profit seems to be taken up. The compensation begins to shrink in your imagination, and all kinds of rationalizations help you to explain that the effort was really yours, that this person's participation was not that decisive, and so forth. However, you're still not convinced. You know that you would like to reward the person, acknowledging the impulse of gratitude and livelihood as it first struck you, but you can't. With one hand in your pocket and the other on your heart, you know that you're up against something very serious. If you don't take the situation in hand, you will be acting like a nothing. If you act half-heartedly, or hesitantly, you will be a fool. If you use the power of your pocket to consider only yourself and reward this person a fraction less than what is due to him, you will be wicked. And if you manage to hand over the correct amount, openheartedly, you will be righteous.

Behaving like a nothing, we destroy the world. When we don't take a stand, we create situations and emotions that are ever more harmful. This evasion undermines our capacity to enjoy and to experience giving. The Market gains nothing through this attitude. The fool, on the other hand, loses himself in the moralistic sermon that is dictated by his pocket. He tries to justify his actions to himself, while knowing deep inside that he is crooked and afraid of going any deeper. He'll end up leaning to one side or the other. Furthermore, his approach is not sincere, but a result of external pressures or internalized repression. The fool will be tremendously unhappy in his decision either way. He will feel that he's been wronged in the transaction and that he has wronged his partner. The Market gains nothing from this but impoverishment.

The wicked are the winners in the material dimension—and the beggars of the other worlds. This is the stance that we most fear when the beggar asks us for money. We fear being wicked and leaving the transaction in an inverted situation—as beggars in other worlds. The wicked are anti-ecological and multiply their wealth in only one dimension, minimizing the gain of the Market. The wicked are, to the Market, a step above the nothings and the fools. This is because the wicked show their cards face up. They make their behavior clear to everyone. Their attitude allows for change and amends because their poverty is real and palpable. The wicked may not know the way out, but they know, at least, where they stand.

The righteous are the masters of the pocket. They are "fools" who are not really fools at all. In other words, they manage to see in this bubbling cauldron of morality/ethics/dignity, aside from the social repression, a Market that is real. Because they know the way, the righteous push onwards through sticky paths of values, untangling themselves from the sticky tentacles of prejudice, destroying the obstacles to sublimation, and resisting the temptation of rewards. The righteous settle in a territory from where they can see things with a dose of irony.

And this irony affords them a glimpse of a more all-encompassing reality. Their peace of mind is different from that of the fool, whose equanimity is falsely based on the belief that his abstractions will magically reveal themselves to be concrete rewards. The peace of the righteous derives from their steps firmly rooted in reality, guided by vision and not by prognosis. The righteous understand what kind of Market we're in—they invest and recover their investments.

We have seen that the wicked are also an important element, because they expose the Market to the possibility of being fixed and corrected. We can learn a lot from them. The Baal Shem Tov (also known as the Besht) made a commentary on this based on the following statement from the *Mishnah:* "In relation to donations there are four attitudes: (1) the person who wants to contribute but doesn't want others to; (2) the person who expects others to contribute but doesn't contribute himself; (3) the person who gives and expects others to do so too; and (4) the person who doesn't contribute and doesn't wish others to contribute either." The Besht said:

"The last case may seem inappropriately listed side by side with attitudes related to giving, as it doesn't result in any form of contribution. If this is so, there would be only three possible attitudes. Why, then, do we have four? Light is known to us because there is darkness; knowledge because there is ignorance; justice because there is wickedness; pleasure because there is pain; remembrance because there is oblivion. One is the chair upon which the other sits. In the same way, noncharity is the chair upon which the generous sit."

Within each of us there is a nongiver, a nonperceiver of these other cycles of return who can help us learn.

Learning from the Thief

Let's return to the scene where we have our hand in our pocket and there's a beggar at our car window. What are our interests in this interaction? We want to do what's right and just in order to avoid losses in larger cycles of return. We want to honor and safeguard who we are at that moment by avoiding false morals or ideals. We don't want to leave our heart entangled in this situation—we want to experience it whole, and get it over and done with. We want to be true to what we see and to how far we see. But the pocket is dark, and we're dealing with evil impulses.

Evil impulses are all around us and are essential elements in shaping our lives. Jewish tradition says that if it weren't for the evil impulse *(yetzer ha-ra)*, we would all starve and no children would be conceived. The evil impulse is the raw material with which we build our self-knowledge. It reveals our intimate behavior, which we disguise not only to the outside world but also to ourselves. When talking about the Market and dealing with the pocket, we use the thief to symbolize our evil impulse. The thief's inclinaton is towards stealing things from people. He can steal from a beggar, the Market, or from himself. But if there has been theft, in the medium and long term, everyone will have been robbed.

There are essentially two dangerous evil impulses: one that pushes us to find excuses for our behavior (like the fool) and one that drives us to run away from situations (like the nothing). About the first impulse, Rabbi Shmelke tells us:

"Don't try to find fault in a poor person who asks you for help as an excuse for not helping him. Don't look for his faults, saying, 'Such a strong man . . . couldn't he work?'—because if you do, God will look for faults in you also and will certainly find many of them. Remember that the mistakes of the person who is begging for your help have already been paid for through his misery, while yours are still with you."

To help or not to help, that is still an unresolved question. But excuses are false paths that contribute to the poverty and to the losses of the Market.

As to the second evil impulse—running away or giving in—we learn from the Berdichever Rabbi, who learned from a thief:

The Rabbi of Berdichev traveled from city to city raising funds for poor people, but he was only meagerly successful. Regretting the time he had wasted, he decided not to get involved with this kind of venture in the future. When he returned home, he saw that a policeman was flogging a thief who had been caught redhanded. The rabbi paid the thief's bail, and when they set him free, he asked the thief if he had learned his lesson and would thenceforth never steal again. The thief answered immediately: "So what if I was flogged? This time I was unlucky, but next time things will be different."

"I should never forget this answer," thought the Berdichever to himself. "In the same way that I wasn't successful this time, I'm sure that next time things will be different."

The Berdichever learns to draw from the same motivation that the evil impulse draws from. In fact, this is the only way to avoid giving in to the impulse—by learning through it. The Maggid ("Preacher") of Mezeritz used to say that we should learn the following qualities from a thief: (1) if once he doesn't succeed, he never gives up; (2) his companions act with the utmost comradeship among themselves; (3) he places his very life in danger to get what he wants; (4) what he gains for himself he sells for little reward; (5) he is patient in misfortune; and (6) he loves his job above any other. Perseverance, fraternity, courage, detachment, tolerance for frustration, and dedication are antidotes distilled from the very poison that harms the Market.

In a moment of interaction, in any situation where there is doubt, never forget the medium- and long-term cycles of return. This is fundamental in order to avoid the evil impulses that drive us to excuses and indifference. If you feel an interaction coming on, count to three. Try to understand that what happens between you and your partner is not only a private situation between the two of you. The following story illustrates this better.

A rabbi was traveling in a coach when the coachman stopped alongside a field where there were various bags of wheat piled up beside the road. He called to the rabbi: "Watch the road, and if anyone sees me, yell!"

When he began to gather the bags, he heard the rabbi yell. He dropped everything and ran off as fast as he could. A few minutes later he looked back and didn't see anyone. "Why did you lie to me, Rabbi?" asked the coachman.

"But it is true, my friend," answered the rabbi. "I yelled because you were being seen . . . seen by He Who lives in the Heavens and is present everywhere."

The *Mishnah* is even more precise and gives us step-by-step instructions on how to deal with our evil impulses in interactions: know (1) where you are coming from, (2) where you are going, and (3) whom you must answer to. In other words: understand the Market deeply. Remember that in each of these infinite cycles of return there is an Eternal Eye that sees everything, an Ear that hears all, and a Book where everything is recorded.

The Art of Ownership

One of the most sophisticated ways to serve the Market is through a deep understanding of the concept of ownership. The Cosmic Market is a constant flow of rights and temporary ownership that makes life possible. And whoever interferes with this essential flow is creating trouble. For example, a person who disrespects the ap-

propriate exchange of food with his environment becomes overweight. He retains in his organism more than
he needs.

In the world of economics we can say that if we
hold on to power or ownership for longer than would be
natural, we are enriching ourselves in this dimension in
an abnormal way. In doing this, we hold back the flow
and become sick. We become "overweight" in the material dimension and must deal with all the costs related
to this.

If we preserve the circulation of property and
avoid stemming the flow of livelihood, we quickly find
ways in which to renew our wealth. In this sense, knowing when to let go of something and when to give presents is an important tool.

Rabbi Zalman Schachter-Shalomi recounts that
one Saturday when he was out walking wearing his
prayer shawl, he was approached by a person who was
impressed by its colors. This person's reaction was so
intense and spontaneous that Reb Zalman offered him
the shawl as a present. The person tried to refuse, but
Reb Zalman wouldn't hear of it. Not that he could easily
part with his shawl, but he had realized that this person
had breached the limits of desire in such a way that
there had been a subtle change in the "right of ownership." Reb Zalman could have kept the shawl, but he
didn't want to—it no longer belonged to him. Better
still, the best benefit he could derive from his property
at that moment was by offering it as a gift. Aware of this

transitional moment, Reb Zalman maximized his gain with respect to the shawl—he made a good *gesheft*.

What I wish to make clear is that the righteous don't simply surrender their belongings, but they do realize when something that belongs to them will represent greater gain if it's no longer theirs. This is related to cycles of greater radii, where the vision of those who are still held back by ownership cannot reach.

If we knew how to do this always, we would be the best of investors. We would let go of our belongings when they were most valuable, most capable of generating pleasure and reward for us.

Rabbi Naḥman once housed a poor traveler in his home. The next morning, however, he discovered that his guest had left, taking with him the rabbi's coat. When Rabbi Naḥman arrived at the synagogue, a young man approached him and said, "Rabbi, a few moments ago I saw a man wearing a coat just like yours. At first I wasn't sure if the coat was yours, but now that I see you without it, I am sure."

"And how did the coat suit him?" asked the rabbi.

"It suited him well," replied the young man.

"Then let him keep it. He is a very poor man, and the winter has been hard."

Those who don't understand this are startled by certain attitudes that are inexplicable within the frame of reality that we build and accept. An example of this is the case of Rabbi Zbarazer, who once, upon returning home, realized that his house was being burgled. He stood still for a few moments and then murmured to the thieves, "I don't want to be held accountable for this sin, so I give all of this to you as a present."

At one point, Rabbi Zbarazer saw that they were carrying away a jar containing chemical products, so he approached one of them and said, "You may take this, but be careful with the contents of this jar, or you'll hurt yourselves."

For some people, this behavior might be considered a case of extreme passivity, but it wasn't. Rabbi Zbarazer was not a saint who wanted to absorb all human errors and let the burglars go scot-free. He realized, though, that the act that he was witnessing was already irreversible, and that his ownership of his belongings had reached its limit. Thus, before the status of the situation transformed into "theft," at the last moment he converted his belongings into a "gift."

Rabbi Zbarazer conforms to the flow. Not all situations call for a solution of this kind. But this kind of solution accepts the incredible paradox of our twisted Market, in which wrong methods (theft) sometimes help to recover the balance of our society. Rabbi Zbarazer makes the right economic decision when he realizes that for that stolen property, there was already an ownership taking precedence over his, the ownership of tzedakah. This is what he sees, and in seeing this he becomes part of the current that really determines what belongs to whom and for how long.

As Moishe the Kabbalist used to say, when something is yours, nobody can take it from you. And when something is no longer yours, it can be dangerous to hold on to it. Learning to enjoy ownership up until almost the last minute is what distinguishes the true hero, the master of the nonconsumerist era that will one day be inaugurated in our world. Being close to God, the mystical union of *devekut* (cleaving or attachment), is an experience in which we awaken to the fact that "ownership" doesn't encompass the experience of "being." Possessions are nothing more than the material outcome of our insecurity and represent the most concrete form of control we can exert as human beings. Even our body is included in this craving for control. Knowing how to let go at the right time, not a moment too soon nor a moment too late, is a sacred art.

6

LIVING IN THE
MATERIAL WORLD

God is seated and He builds staircases. . . .
—*Midrash Rabbah*

What Do Rabbis Know about Money?

Why would rabbis be qualified to serve as counselors
where money and Market are concerned? Should we
trust someone who proposes to give advice when that
person has no practical experience on a given subject?
And where does the experience come from that lends
rabbis their credibility in these matters?

This question is brought up in the following commentary. The Rabbi of Sassov said, "We read in the
Talmud: The rabbis didn't know the meaning of the
verse *Rest your load on the shoulders of God and He will
support you* [Psalms 55:23], until a traveling salesman
explained it to them: 'Rabbis receive a fixed monthly

salary and hence they don't understand very well the meaning of trust in God. The tradesmen, however, for whom livelihood is not guaranteed, depend constantly on divine cooperation. They understand and appreciate the true meaning of trust in God.' "

Comprehension and insight regarding livelihood are prerequisites for those who deal directly with the flow of livelihood, the ephemeral nature of ownership, and the idiosyncrasies of fortune and success.

The rabbis have, since the Talmudic period at the beginning of the common era, struggled with great difficulty for their livelihood. This often happened because they invested heavily in their education and because their ambitions were tempered with a nonmaterialistic comprehension of reality. At the same time, rabbis were totally involved with the problems of their communities, and among these problems were poverty and difficulties with livelihood. Apart from this, the rabbis saw themselves, like all other individuals, as responsible for the settlement and enrichment of the world. Their attitude could never be neutral, detached from the reality of the Market. Their leadership must aim towards transforming this world and consolidating an ideal Market.

This struggle towards transformation doesn't happen only in books, but in the marketplaces and on the streets, where the possibilities of livelihood and enrichment constantly threaten to impoverish us in other worlds. The effort to maximize gain without depleting our treasures in other worlds is the arena where rabbis serve as consultants. The danger of a transaction is that it is processed in various worlds at the same time, and a "good deal" can only be made when both parties know what they want from the transaction. Rabbis qualified as consultants because they could point out the intricate relationships between ethical and spiritual factors. With this knowledge, they could prevent their clients from being tricked into fake gains that would later on generate huge costs.

Rabbis greatly respect the discernment of those who go out daily to seek livelihood—and especially those who don't lose hope even when faced with the terrible distress of a livelihood that is not forthcoming. This faith and this wisdom cannot be taught through consultancy, but the rabbis can help in the recognition of a reality that goes beyond plenty or lack.

A student once asked the Kotzker Rebbe, "If you rabbis seclude yourselves from mundane and material things, how can you counsel us on these matters?"

The Kotzker answered, "Often one who is detached from the matter sees better than one who watches from inside."

The rabbis see matters from the outside, but they respect the dimension of livelihood in the world of Asiyyah, in its material aspect. Often this is the result of their own experience of poverty and the relationship that this poverty has to the disorganization and destruction of the Market at large. Their respect for the Market, their desire to serve as consultants in the area of financial ethics, and their attempt to clarify the flow of livelihood and the obstacles to it have earned them incredible experience in the line of money.

The Wheel of Success and Failure

> The door of success is labeled ENTRANCE and EXIT.
>
> —*Yiddish saying*

An age-old theory says that the world of livelihood, like life itself, is constantly oscillating between the opposites. Wealth is the result not of constant increase, but rather of judicious abstentions from gain that are less than the overall gain itself. From this imbalance springs everything. Because of this imbalance, livelihood is possible. Livelihood, therefore, is a result of Market and not of work.

In our daily lives, we are led to believe that work itself results in livelihood. This isn't true. Of course, without work, without this tool, livelihood will not come about for us. But livelihood is only possible through the interaction of work with the Market. Investing energy (work) in a favorable environment (Market) not only leads to livelihood, but must also be the formula for the genesis of life. For the earth to make itself a human being—Adam—the Divine Breath was necessary, as was the Garden of Eden. The Breath was the energy, and Eden was a favorable ecological niche or Market possibility. That is why the statement quoted at the beginning of this chapter brings the message "God is seated and builds stairways." Using these stairways, some will fall and some will climb.

We can observe this phenomenon in all levels of return. In smaller cycles, we are subject to the laws of the small Market. As a jeweler friend of mine explained:

"It happens, for example, that I buy a stone for a thousand dollars, and between the time of acquisition and sale, the value of the stone drops in such a way that it can be bought on the market for five hundred. Its selling price, therefore, can't go over eight hundred. Many people wouldn't sell, thinking: 'Buy it for a thousand and sell it for eight hundred? Only if I were crazy!' But I sell. The market allows me to. I sell the stone for eight hundred, buy another one at the market price—five hundred—and continue to have a stone that can recover its original market value of a thousand. In the meantime, I've earned my livelihood of three hundred."

This person knows how to yield to momentary losses in order to extract his livelihood from the Market. Have those who are considered successful never made a bad deal? Of course not. Part of the *gesheft* is the detachment from holding on to each penny. A *gesheft* is the possibility of making constant entrances and exits in such a way that what remains, and either moves through our lives or exists as livelihood, is satisfactory. Such understanding can be related to the saying of Rabbi Naḥman of Bratslav: "The fall is a necessary part of the climb" *(Yeridah tzorekh aliyah)*.

This sentence reveals an essential aspect of livelihood: the direct connection between success and failure. In long-term livelihood, in less immediate cycles of return, our "failures" (falls) are part of our success (rise). When we consider the Market within a broad framework, we see that it must account for the whole and not only the partial livelihood of one individual or of a group. This "whole," this interconnection, resembles a wheel: the side that rises does so while the opposite side falls. The highest point signals the beginning of the fall, and the lowest point means we're beginning to climb again. Thus, falling is an essential part of the rising mechanism.

This is the logic that the Nobel Prize–winning Israeli writer S. Y. Agnon uses to describe the magic that commands livelihood in his short story "Rise and Fall." Through this story we can contemplate the rhythm and the flow of livelihood—a flow that is much like the wheel of fortune, which, to be whole, to be Market, demands that what is on the top must descend and what is on the bottom must rise. Thus advances the chariot of fire that brings the future and indeed creates the future.

In his story, Agnon tells of a very rich man who has everything, including a wonderful large family, with a son-in-law who devotes himself entirely to study and who makes him very proud. Once, while going to a fair carrying a lot of money, the rich man asks the driver to stop on the way so that he can attend to a call of nature. He then continues on his way. When he is already far from the place where he had stopped, which was a busy area that everyone going to the fair passed through, he realizes that he has lost his purse with all his money in it. Certain that he will never recover it, he remains at the fair, only returning days later. On his way back, he decides, just out of curiosity, to see if the money is still there. And to his surprise, it is. Suddenly, he begins to weep sadly and heavily. From that moment on, his life begins to fall apart: he loses his money, his wife goes mad, and little by little his family is shattered. The man is bereft of everything, totally destitute and humiliated. The story ends when, finding someone who takes pity on him and invites him to share a Sabbath dinner, he goes to the bathhouse to prepare himself. There, in a quarrel with some beggars, he sees his clothes torn in such a way that now he cannot even get to his benefactor's house for dinner. At this moment, naked, dispossessed, and alone in the world, he begins to laugh compulsively.

The sobs in the coach are the sobs of someone who is at the top of the wheel. Discovering that his lost money was still there made the rich man foresee his downfall in the same way that, naked at the bathhouse, he had hit the bottom and from there could only rise.

Knowing how to recognize these cycles helps us to live with the frustrations and depressions brought on by our falls. No one who has ever experienced livelihood in abundance or success in any area is immune to downfalls. On the contrary, the higher up we are, the more we must deposit as security for the moments of descent. We must make these deposits in riches of the soul so that during our falls we may be warmed by faith in the recurring rise. We must learn to share enthusiasm over the fact that the wheel is turning, and not go into spirals of anguish because another fall is approaching.

The biblical story of Job is the blueprint for Agnon's "Rise and Fall." Many times successful people expect hidden explanations for their fall. They experience the illusory ascent as if it were the unfolding of their own reality. Therefore, they resist the fall, when, if they would only relax and slide down, without tiring themselves in efforts to row against the tide, they would realize that the average of pleasure, livelihood, and satisfaction in the turning of the wheel is quite enough (Blessed is the One!). Happy are those who lose without depression, without letting the feeling of going under be tainted by despair.

Rabbi Nahman used his phrase "The fall is a necessary part of the climb" to fight despair. He understood that the experience of reaching the end of the line was in itself a mystical one. Those who experience the top of the wheel and know the greatness of the Market and the wonders that the Eternal One made possible, as well as those who, crazed by difficulties and suffering, touch their feet to the bottom of the well and realize the Market guarantees available to them—both experience moments of gratitude and satisfaction.

And if people complain about this reality where there must be a summit and an initial downfall, let them remember: Blessed is the One who made fate like a wheel, for He gave the well a bottom and made it such that the strength of what rises supports whatever falls.

The Market exists to contemplate the possibility of life, interdependence, and interconnection. Our individual and collective behavior reinforces or weakens the rims of this wheel. And the possibility of spinning depends upon these rims. The floor where this wheel spins, the inertia that pushes it up and down—these are the only things we can count on. (Blessed is the One who warranties livelihood!)

Knowing What to Ask For

When you go out into the world of the Market, it's a good idea to know what you're looking for. When we go out to buy a certain electronic gadget, we should be aware of the cost-benefit ratio, of which functions will be important to us and which not, the best brand, the best price, and so on. In other words, whoever goes out into the Market would do well to know a little about what he or she is getting into.

In Jewish tradition, this knowledge is one of the most important elements, taking precedence even over wealth itself: What do we want wealth for? What do we want and why? This is the great question. On the most solemn day of the Jewish calendar, Yom Kippur—the Day of Atonement—Jews gather for a whole day to pray. All this exhausting effort aims at distilling a few moments of absolute sincerity when we stand face to face with our Maker. We describe this holiday period as "The Days of Awe," and it is indeed an awe-inspiring experience because of the responsibility involved in having to account for our pleas. What do we want? If you were to have an appointment with the Mayor or the Governor, you might spend days studying and preparing what to say, and above all, what to ask for. If your request is vague, such as simply "Help me," you won't get very far. In prayer, the most frightening thing is to be face to face with God and not know what we really want. In our daily lives we face situations that demand the same precision of objectives, and our frustration is huge when we feel an opportunity slipping through our fingers and it's our own fault. When we don't know what we want, we hesitate and the opportunity passes us by, carried away by the dynamic flow of livelihood.

When we don't know what we want, we become incapable of promoting our own livelihood. Large fortunes are often decimated because the new generation of heirs no longer has a clear objective in livelihood.

If you know what you want and why you want it, your path towards livelihood is unimpeded and you have nothing to worry about. Unlike someone who struggles obsessively to get rich, when you know what you want, you reduce your effort and gather from each moment the available opportunities. The following story will help illustrate this:

A king, wishing to please his most loyal subjects, granted each one a wish. Some asked for honor and power, others for fortune. But one of them said: "My wish is to speak to the King three times a day."

Three is the number of times a day that Jews pray

(morning, afternoon, and evening), and the King with whom we seek an audience is the Creator himself. For the person who knows what to ask for, many doors will open.

Know, therefore, what you want. The great secret is that if you know how to ask for what you should ask for, and if you perfect yourself to the point of knowing the direction towards which you want to drive your efforts in the Market, your wish will be granted as soon as you formulate it. This is incredible magic: if you ask precisely, what you ask for will *already* have been granted you. This is because what we need and desire most is not in the dimension of ownership, but in the dimension of self-knowledge. Those who know how to prioritize their needs have already been granted their wish, for they know what they need the most. Obtaining what we desire is a possibility in the Market of Creation, and searching for it is a fair search. There is nothing that we want that cannot be obtained. The great problem is when we seek to satisfy the wrong needs, mistakenly prioritized, or when the high price of what we are pursuing proves it not to be the true objects of our desire. We waste our requests when we limit them only to the dimension of ownership. And this is the reason many people doubt the effectiveness of prayer. The Baal Shem Tov explained this in the following way:

"When a person prays only for material gains (minimizing his own expectations), his pleas and efforts are wasted. This is because a curtain is drawn between him and God, as a result of material things having been brought into the domain of the spirit. Therefore, his prayers will not be answered."

People who don't know what they want, and what kind of wealth it is that they are investing so much hope in, are wasting their time. This is typical of those who know the *price* of things but don't know what they're *worth*. They pay high prices for objects of little value and offer ridiculously small bids for valuable things, such that, if they knew the worth, they would curse themselves for the opportunities constantly lost. When we don't know what we want, we can't invest, and the Market, instead of bringing livelihood, will drain our time and vitality.

When we know what we want, we can support ourselves easily. Another story of the Besht talks about this.

Once, before he became famous, the Besht didn't have enough money for the Sabbath dinner. The night before, he went to a wealthy man's house, knocked on the door, and left without waiting for a reply. The man got out of bed, dressed quickly, and went after the Besht. When he caught up with him and saw his ragged clothes, he remarked, "If you came to me for help, why did you leave?"

The Besht answered, "When a person is born, his livelihood is born with him. His imperfections, however, cause it to be held back despite his efforts. As each person's imperfections vary in size, the effort that is needed is also different. I believe that my life, far from worldly and material things, allows me to earn a living easily, and that is why I knocked on your door. After I made this effort, I trusted that God would grant me livelihood, and to me it makes no difference if it comes from you or from someone else."

This exaggerated story is proportional to the Besht's own exaggerated character. It was as if he stood at the frontier between humans and saints, and, as such, he needed the minimum to obtain livelihood—desiring it was enough. The saint or the ideal *tzaddik* (righteous person) is beyond livelihood. He is, in fact, livelihood itself. The closer we are to becoming useful and ecologically functional in all worlds, the closer we are to becoming our own livelihood. In this process of "self-supplying," everything comes to us in the correct measure and at the correct time. I insist that this does not reflect a passive stance such as "Be good and everything will be guaranteed." Being good isn't a theoretical abstraction, but a route within the Market. It means being a good negotiator, being honest, and not being a predator in your transactions with other people, other living beings, and the universe itself. Livelihood is a variable only for those who live in harmony with the environment, for those who sanctify themselves through their *gesheftn*, their business deals. These people don't seek out livelihood; livelihood seeks *them* out in an attempt to fulfill its purpose—to support.

This is not an attempt to simplify faith, but an insight open to us all in various moments of our lives. Happiness is when we transform ourselves into livelihood, when we *become* livelihood. And we've all experi-

enced this at one time or another. We've all done something, even if only during our romantic adolescence,
that was absolutely pleasurable and had great potential
for livelihood. The artist, but not the employee, knows
what I'm talking about. The artist realizes that her work
makes her a part of the One, involves her in a mystical
relationship with the world. This kind of livelihood goes
beyond mere survival, is a vehicle of health, and contributes to this universe by enriching it.

These moments in which we become livelihood are
slippery. They elude us, they come and go, but it is
through them that we can steal a glance at the wheel of
fortune. They come and we rise; they go and we fall.
We ground our experience of falling on our belief in a
new climb. Falling is the human condition that makes
for rising again. Much of our livelihood is fueled by
nostalgia, the recollection of our rises and falls. Assur-
ance comes when we understand that livelihood is cy-
clic and that all worlds interact. And the despair we
sometimes feel comes from watching the apparent lin-
earity of this rise and fall. To try to return to the top by
reversing the rotation of the wheel means, physically, to
extend the falling sensation.

To Rabbi Naḥman, those who desperately refuse
to reach the bottom of the well create for themselves
unending drops amid their small victories of ascent.
May God have compassion on those who are like this
and on the part of us that behaves like this.

Such is the world of Asiyyah, the concrete world.

Why must we fall in this dimension? Because falling is a necessary part of rising again: *Yeridah tzorekh aliyah!*

Lotteries and Miracles

Once in a while, for some more than for others, people come across situations of easy livelihood, such as lotteries, legacies, and miracles. These phenomena are part of the constant harmonizing of the Market. We should accept them, however, with caution. Not because they necessarily signal the top of the wheel or the beginning of the fall, for livelihood is not mechanical, with loss necessarily following gain. Nor is this caution because the money is not real, but because it wasn't properly taxed with responsibilities. The danger lies in the way we understand these gains. The way we comprehend them determines whether we bring about impoverishment in other worlds or not. Whenever there's a sudden movement in one dimension of livelihood, we should check whether the interconnections between the different worlds are balanced.

Let's look at this story from the Talmud (*Shabbat* 53b) about miracles.

Once, a man lost his wife in childbirth. The child needed to be fed, but the father didn't have enough money to pay for a wet-nurse. Because of this, a miracle happened for him: his chest opened up and blossomed like a woman's breasts, and he breast-fed his son. Rabbi Yosef commented, "Come and see what a great man this is, for a miracle of this nature happened for him!" Abaye said, "Much to the contrary, my friend. How sad is the story of this man, for whom the order of nature had to be altered."

Abaye had greater vision. Those who count on the Market, on the order established by God, are truly happy. No health is like the health we enjoy when we are functioning as we should. No livelihood is like the livelihood that comes to us in the correct measure. Our ecological niche makes for the possibility of a Market, and this is the miracle we must recognize. In this understanding lies the possibility of broadening the scope of solidarity and interaction. The magical expectation of a miracle and of easy livelihood is for those unhappy people who cannot partake in the greatest of all miracles: day-to-day life. Or, as Rabbi Elazar used to say, "Salvation and livelihood are analogous. . . . In the same way that salvation involves wonders, so does livelihood; in the same way that livelihood happens from day to day, salvation happens from day to day."

Rabbi Shmuel bar Naḥman said: "Livelihood is greater than salvation, because about salvation it is written, *The angel will save you from all evil* (Genesis 48:16); and about livelihood it is written, *You* [God] *open Your hand and* satisfy *all living creatures* (Psalms 145:16). In salvation a 'mere' angel acts; in livelihood, God Himself."

The way we "theologize" about our lives, how we develop our understanding of what happens to us, is fundamental to our well-being in this world of the Mar-

THE KABBALAH OF MONEY

ket. We observed earlier that the arrogant, who see their climb on the wheel of life as the result of pure merit, are unhappy and desperate when falling. A sudden gain in the world of Asiyyah can often reverberate in more subtle worlds of livelihood, worlds that produce depression, apathy, and death impulses.

The greatest safety we have is the trust in the constant miracle of livelihood. Both kinds of miracles, lottery and livelihood, are good and should be seen through one's own life perspective. Unhappy are those people who wait for a miracle, relying upon the disruption of the natural order of Creation. These people are anti-ecological, opportunists, consumerists, and predators. And if they don't realize the sadness they produce by desperately trying to avoid completing the cycle of descent, they may even be holding back the wheel itself.

Partnerships and Contracts

Finding partners in the dimension of Asiyyah is a difficult task. Mostly, partners commit two very common mistakes. The first is not knowing how to ask. In other words, "partners" don't necessarily have the same livelihood objectives. And as we've seen, becoming wealthy is a process that requires sensitivity so as not to obstruct the various dimensions of wealth.

Many times, partners are not clear to one another about their expectations of wealth. This makes the partnership more difficult, because a good partner is one who brings us closer to our hopes in the various worlds.

An interesting story about how to find an ideal partner is told by the Rebbe of Apt:

"Once I lodged at an inn, and I noticed that the owner had two boxes where he kept money. Any money that he earned, he would divide equally between the two boxes. I was curious about the meaning of this, and, telling him who I was, I questioned him on the subject. He answered, 'Not a long time ago I lost all my life savings in a venture and I was about to lose my inn as well. My wife then advised me to get a partner and I went into town to look for one. As I was traveling through the forest, it occurred to me to ask God to join in this partnership with me, and I promised to offer His gains to charity. I prayed for a few moments, and then I found some money on the ground along the path. I took this as a sign of our deal, and since then I have kept strictly to our oral contract.' I then commended that man on the simple trust he reposed in God, and I blessed him."

The innkeeper's approach is not a bad idea. Before entering any partnership, try admitting that there is a previous partnership that must be settled. Strictly accounting for this partnership is doubtlessly a very healthy attitude towards the maintenance of all other partnerships in the world of Asiyyah.

The second problem concerns contracts. Nobody can ever be rich, by definition, without understanding the art of drawing up good contracts. We should be truly

obsessive about this. Normally, we have a naive, romantic idea about business relations: we feel that it's
shameful or disrespectful to want to nail down the precise details in a written agreement, or to use witnesses.
But much to the contrary, doing so represents the greatest form of respect there is. In fact, any other practice
would be "placing a stumbling block before the blind."
If there were no careless contracts, perhaps marriages
wouldn't dissolve, families wouldn't fight, and societies
wouldn't disintegrate. Because of this, contracts are sacred for the rabbis. What is written down here reflects
up there, in the higher worlds.

And if anyone still has doubts, just think of the
time, energy, and suffering that we waste because of
bad contracts. What is *not* written down here also reflects up there. If with part of His time God builds staircases, with the other part He draws up perfect contracts. This universe itself is an example of conformity
to a wonderful contract. We Jews call this contract
Torah.

The greatest enemy of a contract is the immaturity
that embarrasses people when the time comes to establish rules for their transactions. We usually think that it
demonstrates a lack of trust or solidarity to want to settle these interactions in detail. But the righteous know
the limits of solidarity and are able to draw up careful
contracts. The Rabbi of Berdichev always conducted a
test that warned him against these dangers:

One day the Berdichever was sought out by the
butcher of the city, who asked him: "Are you a *shoḥet*

[ritual slaughterer]? I need a *shohet* immediately, and I can't wait for the one who comes by here once a week."

The Berdichever answered in the affirmative. The butcher promised him additional payment if the job was done quickly. But the Berdichever continued, "I will do it on condition that you lend me twenty talents, which I promise to return to you promptly."

"No!" exclaimed the butcher. "I can't lend money to someone I barely know!"

"You have just shown me that you are a person who could cause a lot of problems," said the rabbi. "You refuse to trust me with your money because you don't know me, and at the same time you're willing to contract me, presuming that I am a *shohet,* without asking me for any credentials. How do you know that I'm not an unethical man?" The butcher then realized what he was doing.

To make sure there is trust, often we must use the Berdichever test. In summary, this test uses concrete conditions, such as a loan without guarantees, to reveal the true trust involved in each transaction. And it exposes the subjectivity with which we make our contracts and points to our need to perfect this art.

We should imitate our Creator, of Whom we are the likeness and resemblance. If His time is dedicated to contracts, then our time should also be. Make clear "contracts" for everything and everyone, and avoid carelessness. Otherwise every partnership in life may bring ruin.

"Getting Involved"

Why do people get involved with one another?

To answer this question, let's consider, for example, the following situation. We're driving down the street on a Sunday, enjoying our free time, when we witness an accident. Suddenly, we find ourselves involved and forced to stop. We assist the victims, coping with all the violence of the situation, and drive them to the hospital. When we later stop to evaluate our losses of time, pleasure, and even money, we ask ourselves: Why did I get so intensely involved? Someone else might have casually taken a side road, never even known about the accident, and gone on enjoying the day. A split second or a few feet can mean the difference between being involved or not.

The rabbis illustrate involvement with the ordinary situation of finding a lost wallet. The money in it doesn't belong to us, even if it's only cash and there is no identification of the owner. From the moment we see the wallet onwards, we become responsible for safeguarding that money and for returning it. But why should we? If we hadn't found the wallet, we'd be exempt from this burden. But once we've seen the wallet, we become hopelessly involved with the situation. Involvement is sudden, instantaneous, and offers no way out. And when we do get involved, when we interact, we must once again choose one of the four responses to interaction: we can be nothing, foolish, wicked, or righteous.

So involvement is a law of life. Living means experiencing life "situations." We move constantly from one life situation to another. Those situations that fill us with good feelings we call opportunities, and those that we consider bad incidents we try to reject and ignore. But in both cases, the same thing is happening: we are interacting. This is why we need to draw up contracts between ourselves and our conscience.

The best contract is the righteous kind, whereby we enjoy life to the exact measure by honoring its limitations.

There is no way out of an interaction, except death. People who kill themselves are often those who gave in to despair when facing these four possibilities of interaction and who chose to escape from the interaction itself. Some, like the rabbis, believe that even in death we cannot avoid the four options.

Debts

What are debts? What kind of interaction are they?

Let's try to differentiate between debt and the kind of theft that entails withholding what belongs to another, as discussed in chapter 4. The case of theft referred to deliberately withholding something that belongs to someone else and that we are in a position to return. Here, in the case of debt, we are unable to return what we borrowed. This inability, according to the rabbis, often extends beyond the material dimension.

A man once complained to the Rabbi of Porissov

that he was drowning in debts. The rabbi advised him: "Of each penny of profit that you earn, set aside part for the payment of your debts. When it's clear to the Heavens that you really want to pay them back, then you'll have help to do that."

The Rabbi of Porissov, in this very cunning way, shows us that our debts, especially when we're drowning in them, often reflect a deeper, more subtle desire *not* to pay them back. If we make the effort to repay our debts into a habit, then we will find the means to do it.

The same is true of people who lend money to others who suffer from this problem. In this interconnected world it would be fairer to help debtors by not lending them money. The following age-old Jewish anecdote, despite its prejudiced undertone, refers to an important Market reality about debts.

Isaac owed money to his neighbor Jacob. The night before the payment was due, Isaac tossed and turned in his bed, making it impossible for his wife to sleep. At one point, she sat up angrily and asked, "Isaac, what's the matter?"

Isaac answered, "I have to pay back an enormous debt to Jacob tomorrow, and I don't have the money."

His wife, who was by now quite upset, didn't think twice. She went to the window and yelled, "Jacob, my husband Isaac owes you money that is due tomorrow and he doesn't have the means to pay you back. He couldn't sleep and has already done his part—now it's your turn not to sleep!"

This world is a giant net, and when we take on too

many debts, we are being financed either by those who aren't skilled in the art of drawing up contracts or by those who encourage compulsive indebtedness. Third world countries learned this from the industrialized countries they owed money to. The Market is such that when a debt is too large, we have only to remind the creditor of the money he is owed for him to break down. When the interconnection is this all-encompassing, all excess, even in a debt, means a double chore for us— that of lending the money out and of later having to make concessions in order to make repayment possible.

Lending and borrowing are two essential elements in the Market, and they are described metaphysically in the *Ethics of the Fathers* (3:20):

> Everything is given on a pledge, and a net is spread for all the living; the shop is open; the shopkeeper sells on credit; the ledger is open; and the hand writes; and everyone who wishes to borrow, let him come and borrow; but the collec-tors make their rounds every day, and collect peo-ple's payment with or without their consent; for they have proof to rely on.

"Having proof to rely on" means a guarantee not only for the creditor but, above all, for the person who borrows. And we trust that the shop will remain open and the possibilities of exchange and business will continue to grow in the universe.

Loans and Interest

The world in which we live is a world of loans. Life itself is made of "capital" lent to us by our parents, which they borrowed from "intergenerational" funds. Loans are acts of generosity that date back to before we were born and that make survival possible. We try to imitate this primary act of affection by attempting to reconstruct in the Market the same kind of vitality that we experience in our own lives. In *Exodus Rabbah* we read the following commentary.

> Observe how all of creation borrows from one another:
> The day borrows from the night, and the night from the day.
> The moon borrows from the stars, and the stars from the moon.
> Knowledge borrows from comprehension and comprehension from knowledge.
> The Heavens borrow from the earth and the earth from the Heavens.
> Thus it is also with human beings, with a single difference: all these others borrow without ending up in court.

A loan, in Jewish tradition, is a kind of "justice" (tzedakah). Only through this kind of loan can we fight real poverty. In the same way that we tax our production surplus to help combat world poverty, we should also tax our surplus capital. That's why the Bible establishes: "If you lend money to the poor among My people, do not behave to them like a creditor—do not charge interest" (Exodus 22:24).

During many centuries of misery and persecution, the Jews have had a strong ally in survival and livelihood: their lending system, which sometimes even meant institutions that loaned money free of interest. Loans in the form of tzedakah bring many advantages to the Market. The first is the commitment made by both the person who taxes himself by lending and the person who obliges himself to pay back the loan. There is an element in this debt that is favorable to the enrichment of the world. The second advantage is that this loan makes for a tzedakah free from its number one enemies: shame and humiliation. In Jewish tradition, shame is the only nonphysical pain that is comparable to misery. In the *Sefer ha-Ḥasidim* (Book of the Pious), a thirteenth-century work on ethics, we read about this:

> Ruben was an honest man who asked to borrow some money from Simon. Simon agreed at once and added, "In fact, I'm giving you this as a present." Ruben was so ashamed that he never borrowed money from Simon again. In this case, it clearly would have been better to lend than to give.

The biblical verse from Exodus quoted above, as it is written, gives rise to many questions and presents various problems to the Market of loans. Initially, we could interpret "Do not behave to them like a creditor" to mean that no loan could be collected after its due date expired, if the debtor was unable to pay it back.

The rabbis are very careful about this. Acts of tzedakah should not be confused with *gemilut ha-sadim*—good deeds or acts of kindness. We should never mix these two separate worlds. Justice (*din*) and kindness (*ḥesed*) are two distinct dimensions, and the balance of our world and of our Market depends on this distinction. Confusing these two dimensions is a mistake often made by the foolish, or by those who insist on transforming "something into nothing." When we don't know how to separate justice and kindness, we make this world into a more chaotic place, and our attitude can be compared to corruption and bribery, even if our intentions are good.

When we lend money, we can eventually choose to pardon the debt, but this should be done separately and independently from the loan. This forgiveness can therefore be an act of kindness (*gemilut ḥasadim*) but it can never be both an act of tzedakah (justice) and *gemilut ḥasadim* at the same time.

Let us emphasize this important concept: justice and compassion work together, but must remain independent from each other. When kindness overlaps into justice or justice overlaps into kindness, we weaken the Market and risk the downfall of society, either through too much strictness and inflexibility or as a result of frivolity and thoughtlessness. Happy is the person who lives in a society where there is harmony between justice and compassion. When pushed into the same space, they are contradictory. One works through closed eyes—the blind and impartial eyes of justice. The other works through open eyes—the eyes of compassion, which favor our fellow human beings. You can't have your eyes open and closed at the same time. And yet our vision is made of both light and absence of light.

Another dangerous belief is that the Market does not accommodate any kind of interest. This contradicts modern market practices that aim not at eliminating interest rates but at reducing them to their lowest (and more real) possible figures.

Interest rates are compensation for two possible kinds of loss that can result from a loan. The first kind of loss is proportional to the time the sum remains on loan. When we lend money, it becomes unavailable to us for a time. In other words, we are like a worker who has her salary withheld and is unable to use it. This compensation is designed to cover our loss of freedom of investment and acquisition. The second kind of loss is proportional to the risk that we take on when we lend money. We risk the loan never being paid back if, for example, the business in which the money was invested goes bankrupt. This is how the financial market works: the more agile a market is, the greater its money's potential for generating more money. The greater the risk in a loan, the higher the interest rates—compensation for handing over your capital—of the Market. And this seems fair, at least from a simplistic point of view.

The rabbis would secretly agree with this. However, like any contemporary individual or institution whose job it is to control the Market, they take it upon themselves to reduce the interest, or even eliminate it whenever possible.

The rabbis provide several insights into the dangerous nature of uncontrolled interest rates. The Hebrew word for interest used in the Bible is *neshekh,* which literally means a "bite." The medieval French commentator known as Rashi points out that a snake bite, for example, is at first only uncomfortable, but later it swells, becomes serious, and causes much suffering. In the same way, interest is at first only uncomfortable, but with time it becomes a fatal poison to individual or institutional economies.

Interest carries potential for unreal growth, and when this happens, we produce unreal money: namely, a greater quantity of money than would have been generated if the same amount had been invested in the Market. This can develop into a kind of theft that we call inflation. Inflation occurs when various small thefts of this kind burst out and widespread distrust ensues in the Market.

Meir Tamari, in his book *With All Your Possessions,* reminds us that Judaism does not share the Christian notion that money should not generate wealth in the same way that trees, land, or cattle do. To the rabbis, money is part of the incredible wonder of the Market and can, as such, produce wealth, as long as it's real wealth. What money should not do is dictate the pace of this enrichment. That should merely follow the growth of the Market. In other words, money can produce more money only to a level similar in proportion to the wealth that can be produced by trees, land, and cattle or any other areas of the economy considered wealth-producing.

At the same time, the rabbis realize that the practice of lending money without charging interest is of fundamental importance to any society. And it is up to each community to distribute these subsidized loans using any criteria it sees fit. The rabbinical community considered that all Jews were to be included in their criteria, so they forbade loans that charged interest rates among Jews. This criterion has often been considered discriminatory, but it's not. It is simply a special good deed. Just as we contribute to our home teams or to specific causes or groups that are dear to us, Jews traditionally sought to protect one another. And if we recall that in medieval times the Jews were not allowed to own land or other means of production, this doesn't seem such an absurd criterion. One thing was for sure, no one but the Jews themselves would worry about the Jews. So interest-free loans are not a benefit conceded only to a select group, but a generous concession that could not be extended to everyone. This is because our economy cannot function without interest rates, and without them, no one would be interested in lending money and the world would be a more miserable place.

Every market should selectively distribute some of its resources free of interest where it believes it can ease misery and really make a difference. In doing this, in the medium and long term, it will be contributing to its own enrichment.

Real Business

In order to sustain a Market that is geared towards the settlement of the world, we must make constant adjustments that aim at guaranteeing that all business conducted within it is real. We tend, in our day-to-day practice, to corrupt the Market by refusing to acknowledge the interconnections between the various worlds of wealth. Often the agents of the Market themselves, those involved in business, function like "viruses," imposing enrichment only in the material dimension. Combating and restricting these people can be a difficult job. All the wit we use in trying to promote a real economy is counteracted by the equally sophisticated wit of those who are bent on transforming real wealth into immediate wealth. For many centuries, the rabbis have fought an energetic battle of wits against these "business entities" for control of the Market.

It is precisely because interest, dressed up in various misleading guises, has always been the most effective weapon used by these agents in their struggle for control of the Market, that the rabbis chose to fight interest so vehemently. They picked this fight exactly because they knew how important interest was to the Market. With this in mind, the rabbis demanded that loans be transformed into another kind of operation—investment partnerships *(hetter iskah)*.

Using a specific legal mechanism, the person who was lending the money became an investment partner to the person who was borrowing. As such, he shared the success or failure of his partner's financial adventures, collecting part of the profit (which seemed to him like interest). This policy promoted direct contact between the person who was lending the money and the Market reality. In the long run, it's as if the supplier of capital were himself investing in the Market. Using this mechanism, the rabbis managed to transform potential profiteers and middlemen into real investors. In this way, the Market would be adequately remunerating the capital according to its success and its capacity for producing real wealth.

We won't dwell on the details of this mechanism. We are merely interested in this desire of the rabbis not to allow the existence of markets parallel to the Greater Market. The rabbis struggle against the idolatry that conceives "heretical" markets by instead offering people faith in the One Market, which is real and accounts for wealth in all its levels and consequences. All worlds of wealth merge into one Market. And this is a reality that these "business entities" tend to systematically reject.

Prices and Profits

Another element that destabilizes the Market is disparity between supply and demand. In the Bible we read:

"When you buy or sell to your neighbor, you should not cheat one another" (Leviticus 25:14).

Despite the fact that a product's real price when it reaches the Market includes extra costs (transport, storage, etc.), we still see fluctuations from one shop to another. The rabbis determine that if this fluctuation amounts to more than one sixth of the value of the good, then it's classified as cheating *(ona'ah)*. In this case, the deal can be undone within the time required for the product to be priced by a specialist. The objective of this fifteen-hundred-year-old "consumer protection code" is to avoid speculation and unreal wealth. However, according to Maimonides, ona'ah only applies where there is unfairness involved:

> Those who buy and sell fairly cannot be accused of cheating. If a merchant says to a customer, "This article that I'm selling for two hundred is sold on the market for one hundred," and still he chooses to buy, there is no cheating involved. *(Mishneh Torah, Hilkhot Mekhirah* 13:4)

In other words, if merchants are up front about why they sell their goods above the apparent market price, we don't consider it ona'ah. Nevertheless, this variation must be explained based on the additional costs of that product, associated with either rarity or quality. There's one more restriction we must consider: when the price is exaggerated in face of the needs of the consumer. Here again we have ona'ah. A classical case is described in the Talmud.

A fugitive must cross a river, and the boatman, aware of this, charges much more than the usual price. Because he has no other alternatives, the fugitive pays the price. Even if he had been warned by the boatman that this was not the usual price and had agreed to pay anyway, he is still entitled to complain and receive the difference back, because this is ona'ah. In other words, in moments of distress and emergency *(be-sha'at ha-dehak)*, because we have no alternatives, prices no longer represent *gesheftn* (real transactions). This is very different from the situation where a customer has a choice and chooses to buy a more expensive product that has appealed to her, because she trusts either its quality or the guarantee that that particular merchant has offered her.

The rabbis are not interested in controlling the market, and they're not concerned about transactions involving prices above the market price, as long as these are conducted according to the customer's interest. This kind of special interest is encompassed by the Market, despite being very abstract. Unfairness, speculation, and exploitation are what the rabbis fear. They expect transactions to be made using only real values. This is so true that what I have called real money they call *hayyei nefesh* (literally, the corporeality or vitality of the soul), expressing the need to keep body and soul together. This real money is part of the huge cauldron of exchanges and interactions of the universe.

Ona'ah also applies when merchants retail their products below market price by mistake. The customer is permitted to buy the product within the time required for a specialist to ascertain the real price, whereas the merchant has unrestricted time to prove that he has suffered ona'ah.

The element that guarantees the possibility of real transactions in *hayyei nefesh,* "life-money," is free access to information. If both parties have all the necessary information about the market, their decisions will be pertinent and will contribute to the Market's definition. After all, if the ideal consumer, as imagined by the rabbis, knows the value of things in the various dimensions, who better than that person should control their prices?

The Search for a Real Price

Establishing a fair price for things is a task of utmost importance. It is a sacred quest that requires the most sophisticated kind of wisdom and justice available in each generation. So far we have determined prices based on supply and demand. There is another variable, however, to be considered in this relationship, which represents the various interconnected worlds of wealth. The rabbis called this variable *hassagat gevul* (establishing boundaries). Its origin is in a biblical precept (Deuteronomy 19:14) that forbids us to move the boundary markers from someone else's land in order to increase our own.

According to the Bible, this is not just an ordinary

case of theft, for besides being an appropriation of someone else's property, it represents an invasion of that person's livelihood as well. This is because land no longer tended by its true owner constitutes an additional loss. The Bible considers land to be property in a special sense, in that it produces spontaneously and interferes in a more complex way with our wealth.

What this means is that prices reflect not only the product's inherent value, but also its cost responsibilities to the Market. Let's imagine, for example, a product that when manufactured, pollutes our rivers. If, besides the cost of production, we incorporate the cost it represents to the environment, such as the expense of cleaning the rivers, we would be bringing the price closer to its real value. We'd be taking into consideration the externalities, or hidden social costs, that each good carries. We'd also be penalizing the *hassagat gevul* that is a part of the manufacturing process of that product. Someone who doesn't need or doesn't use that good would not have to share the cost of that loss to the environment. The charge for cleaning up the environment that the industries would have to collect to make up for their "invasion of public land" *(hassagat gevul)* would be incorporated into the price of the product.

In other words, each consumer would take on the costs of his acquisitions in as many worlds as he can envision. The advantage is that, if everyone behaved like this, we'd be increasing the scope of justice, rationalizing the prices of the Market, and taxing them with responsibility. Nothing is forbidden to the consumer, so long as he assumes total responsibility for the cost of his ventures.

In a way, we are rehearsing this ideal when we pay our taxes to institutions that organize the social and public domains of our lives. But the rabbis believed that each and every transaction should bear full responsibility for its consequences, and the more these responsibilities are transferred to individuals instead of institutions, the better.

The very definition of a Market is related to this incredible interconnection of everything to everything else. It's impossible to interfere with something here without disturbing something elsewhere and so producing a different form of equilibrium. If we look at things this way, establishing a fair price seems nearly impossible. It demands deep wisdom and knowledge of the interconnections of this universe. Finding that perfectly fair price is such an intricate and worthy life-long job that we could even say that it's the very reason for our existence. The cosmically fine-tuned price would have to consider and prioritize all things according to the infinite correlation of the universe. The true value of something with respect to the larger Market is an element that could lead us even to debrief the universe's innermost secrets. A real value would be an absolute parameter.

This is why the rabbis recommend that we avoid moving too far from society—according to the saying *Al tifrosh min ha-tzibur*, "Don't separate yourself from the community"—or, I would add, from the Market. This is how life teaches us that there are no values independent of the Market, and that prices can only exist within the Market. Outside there are no prices, no values. Light and darkness cannot exist separately; one defines the other. A fair price is part of the definition of all else. In a way, prices or values indicate that we are in the presence of life and vitality. On any planet where there is some form of life, there will be values and prices. Wherever there is life, there will be priorities, and with them arise the dilemmas of the pocket. The decisions that come from the pocket reveal our values and our comprehension of ourselves as human beings. The sum of our pocket-decisions is the basis for real relationships, as real as anything can be. Prices are our reality. They don't reflect what we'd like them to. They reflect a relationship towards the world at a given instant, and in doing that, they take on a particular value.

Prices unearth information from subtle and hidden worlds that lend solidity to reality. Wise people—because they know the importance of collecting as much information as possible when determining prices—can organize their time and establish how they want to "spend" this life. The more certain we are of values, the more precise our prices will be, and the more meaning we'll be lending to life. If we know the prices in life, we avoid the distress of making bad deals.

Unfortunately, however, very few people realize that predatory pricing in the Market results in confusion of values and works against life (she-lo le-ḥayyim).

Dealing with Prices

The rabbis teach us how to deal with the various day-to-day situations related to prices. Here are some examples to illustrate the rabbinical approach.

Rabbi Safra was saying his morning prayers when a client came up to him interested in buying his donkey. Because Jews are forbidden by tradition to interrupt their prayer, he didn't answer. The client interpreted his silence to mean that he considered the offer unsatisfactory, so he upped his price. As the rabbi still didn't reply, he raised his offer even higher.

When Rabbi Safra finished his prayers, he said to the man, "I decided to sell my donkey to you for the first price you offered me, but I didn't want to interrupt my prayers to do business. So you may have it for the first price; I won't accept the higher offers."

Rabbi Safra manages to keep track of the fair price, avoiding the temptation of taking advantage of the situation. Good businesspeople only take advantage of a situation when it's "real." They realize that if the cost of losing faith in the world of exchanges is higher than the temporary advantage gained by closing the deal, the opportunity is a false one.

At the same time, they know that acts of goodwill must necessarily be well thought out in order not to be counterproductive. The Market is no place for gullibility.

Let's look at this example where it becomes obvious that good intentions are not enough:

Samuel was wise, and he was in the habit of storing food when it could be bought cheap. When the prices went up, he would sell his products at lower prices to the poor. Not long after doing just this, he received word from other wise people asking him to stop. Why? Because his habit of storing the goods could in itself be causing the increase in prices, and once they went up, they would stay high.

In order to positively impact the Market, it is essential that we know something of its nature. Just as the sailor knows the sea, its secrets and its tricks, those who circulate in the world of business must know the idiosyncrasies of each world. The material, emotional, intellectual, and spiritual worlds of livelihood are distinct dimensions. Good sailors, like good astronauts, behave with complete awareness that they are surrounded by a reality that is different from the one they experience on land.

The rabbis also worried about the product itself. In the same way that nowadays consumer codes demand that the product be exactly what it's made out to be, the rabbis warned us constantly about weights and measures. In the Bible itself there are two recommendations (in Leviticus and Deuteronomy) that there be a single standard for weights and measures, aside from the obvious reference to the essential honesty in using these standards. The *Mishnah* (*Bava Batra* 5:10) illustrates this point.

> A large store-owner must clean his scales or his measuring stick every thirty days, and a small store-owner may do so once every twelve months.

Rabban Shimon ben Gamliel said the opposite: "A small storeowner should clean his measuring instruments more frequently, because with the lack of use, his scales become dusty and sticky, losing their precision.

"Aside from this, the storeowners should clean out their scales twice a week, polish their weights once a week, and clean out the plates after each weighing."

Of course, the rabbis knew that this was difficult to control. They often asked themselves whether they should warn the population against possible thefts. Rabbi Yohanan said, "It is difficult for me to talk about forged weights, and it is difficult for me to avoid talking about them. If I go into details about the art of weighing, the ugly-minded might use this knowledge. On the other hand, if we don't let them know that we are aware of their tricks and that the populace could come to know about them, then they'll take us for fools and go on doing it." Rabbi Shmuel says that Rabbi Yohanan decided to reveal his knowledge based on a verse of Hosea (7:12): "The wicked will be caught in their own nets."

Information is still our best protection against the "wicked" of the Market.

Prices and Quality of Life

So we see that hidden social costs should be considered so that we may charge each product with its responsibility to the world. In essence, prices determine

the quality of life of a population. In order for prices
to be taxed, we must establish criteria of connections
between the product and the consequences of its production. This is a concept known as *geri delei* (direct
connection) whereby we relate each economic activity
to its responsibilities.

In the Talmud there is an example of *geri delei* that
mentions Papi Yonah, who won a suit against sesame oil
producers working nearby by claiming that their production method caused so much vibration that it shook
his whole house.

Another, contemporary case that is quite illustra-
tive is discussed by Rabbi Meir Abulafia. He established that the people in a neighborhood could demand
the shutdown of any economic activity that generated
traffic in their area. Traffic means two different kinds of
problems: noise pollution and time pollution. In this
case, time pollution, or everyone's loss of time in traffic
jams, was an objective reason for sanctions towards the
economic activity that was causing the problem.

People in a society may choose to share costs,
agreeing, for example, to the price of coping with traffic
in the public streets. However, it could be the responsibility of certain businesses to incorporate the hidden
social costs into the price of their products in order to
ameliorate this situation. A given product might have
its price raised, with the excess to be contributed
towards the construction of traffic alternatives that
avoid time pollution. The usual taxes, in this case,
would only need to cover the overhead costs of road

maintenance. Every person or institution causing time pollution beyond the minimum cost shared by the population in its taxes, would bear the financial burden of this.

Connection criteria are essential for such evaluations, and they should be made part of our culture and our way of thinking. All those who count themselves as part of this huge multinational enterprise of living beings should make the extra effort.

Competition

We have seen so far that for the last two thousand years, the rabbis have believed in a Market economy. They believed that competition concealed the sacred art of establishing prices, Market, meaning, and life. In the *Mishnah* (*Bava Metzia* 4:12) we read about this:

> Rabbi Yehudah said: Merchants should not give almonds to children, because this would encourage the children to buy only at their own shops and create unfair competition. But our sages thought differently and allowed this.
>
> Rabbi Yehudah also used to say that a merchant should not offer products below the market price. But the sages said that if someone behaves like this, his memory should be a blessing.

The limits of competition are drawn from the various concepts that we've mentioned so far such as avoiding theft and *hassagat gevul* (invasion of another person's livelihood) and from our constant effort towards the enrichment of the world. Rabbis also strongly oppose monopolies. In the Talmud, a family is mentioned whose name was to be blotted from memory because they were secretive and obstructed honest competition in their economic activity.

Competition is one kind of interaction in the Market. We should not lose sight of the fact that we are here to *compete* in the literal meaning of the word: "to seek together." In that context, the act of competing is a collective search, a form of cooperation which favors the establishment of an ecosystem that is essential to the Market and to exchange.

7

AGENTS OF
LIVELIHOOD

Luck

> You can have anything, as long as it is not against
> God's will.
>
> —*Yiddish saying*

In Jewish tradition, we say that *a bissale mazel* (Yiddish, "a little luck") makes all the difference. "A pinch of luck is worth more than a pound of gold," goes the saying. But what is luck? A tradition that preaches interconnection and far-ranging responsibilities cannot vouch for an element that means perchance being at the right place at the right time. If it did, it would be admitting the existence of chaotic and random elements in this world. And at the same time that these elements would explain many events that we see through the light of our intellect, they would also corrode our belief in Divine Providence *(hashgaḥa)*. After all, would there be Someone dishing out this luck, or would the dispensation be completely random?

Mazel, translated here as luck, in its Hebrew original meant fate. And fate, according to the Talmud, means that "everything is in the hands of God, except our reverence towards Him." All our decisions, all our free will, is limited to this dimension—to whether we have reverence towards God or not. Our freedom lies only in being able (or wanting) to understand our experiences in this light or not. It is difficult for us to accept that everything except faith is predestined. There is no process in this universe, large or small, complex or simple, that cannot be predicted. Faith, however, is unpredictable. Within this small gap where we choose either to revere God or not, we encounter all the surprises and all the "chances" of the universe. And it is exactly in the physical world that we fight this battle between revering and not revering. Because of the concrete nature of this world, it is here that our faith must be tested. Matter can corrode faith, but it is also the only dimension in which faith can emerge. When we go beyond the objectives, the meaning, and the logic that the physical world offers us, we are generating the raw materials with which we build our faith.

We humans live in a physical environment, where we have access to decision making and free will. And this dimension offers us enough power of decision making that we may recognize and revere an underlying order or not. This is what matters. The luck we are talking about is just a kind of illusion that results when life and this physical environment meet. Being in the right place at the right time is a real possibility in this dimension.

But this is not the luck we mean when we use the word *mazel*. Mazel is a small miracle, a spark of the larger Miracle in which we are immersed, that we can sometimes evoke. Mazel is when we transform segulah, or treasure, into "right place, right time." It's like one of those video games where every thousand points, for example, allow you to disappear from the screen, to become invulnerable or to re-create the scenery as best suits you. But those who play regularly realize that it is best not to use these resources. There are many disadvantages in using them, and the highest scores usually go to players who avoid these extras. And yet sometimes using these bonuses helps us to continue in the game. It's like a bissale mazel. It's good if we have a little luck, and sometimes knowing that we can count on it is a gift in itself.

Wasting too much mazel is worrying, as we saw earlier in the example of the wheel whose highest point is also the beginning of the downfall. That's why we also welcome a little "bad" luck in Jewish tradition. When someone drops a plate and it breaks, we say, "Mazel tov!" (Good luck!). In other words, "It's good that you didn't use up your good luck in keeping that plate from breaking." That would be a real waste.

This is the irony that underlies our gratitude for our small moments of bad luck, which, in a way, increase our overall good luck. Luck is therefore quite relative. It also means having luck at the right time and for the right thing. If we look at things this way, not everyone spots luck when it happens to him. And sometimes what we believe to be good luck is really bad luck.

Often rabbis evoke luck to complement something that will inevitably happen so that it does so without delay or disturbance. In this case, luck is a last-minute effort to speed up something that would happen anyway. This is why we don't idolize mazel, but we welcome it when it comes at the right moment and for the right thing.

If we were to demand a mechanical explanation for mazel, the rabbis would tell us that it's related to the systems of livelihood we discussed before. Mazel is when a need leaves this dimension and goes into other worlds in search of livelihood. When it returns, it surfaces magically. Luck is the materialization of our livelihood when it comes from other worlds into the material dimension. These events surprise us because we don't understand them. A need goes from this world to another in such a way that we cannot follow, and comes back satisfied. This is the discontinuity of cause and effect that we call luck.

But how can we find luck when we need it?

It is possible, and even necessary at times, to call on luck. Rabbi Naḥman used to urge people: "My friends, make use of your treasures." He was trying to point out to us the riches we have in the various worlds and that we don't know how to use. If you understand the interconnection between the various worlds of wealth, then you know the dangers of concentrating all your wealth in one dimension only. And you'll discover that you can transfer these riches from one dimension to the other when necessary.

Doubtless the first step towards calling on luck is being absolutely certain that these resources, these treasures of other dimensions, are real. The following Ḥasidic story may help us understand this.

Rabbi Yitzḥak lived in the city of Cracow and was very poor. For three straight nights he dreamed of a treasure hidden under a bridge in Prague. The dream was so intense that he decided to go to Prague to look for the treasure. When he arrived, he discovered that the bridge was guarded day and night by the king's soldiers. He waited there until the captain of the guard came to ask him what he wanted. Rabbi Yitzḥak told him about his dream.

"You mean to tell me that you believe in such a dream?" laughed the captain. "If I believed in dreams, then I would have traveled to the faraway city of Cracow to find a rabbi, I think his name was Yitzḥak, because I dreamed there was a great treasure buried under his bed!" Rabbi Yitzḥak thanked the captain, went home, and found the treasure under his own bed.

This story reminds us that the true source of all treasures is internal. Our treasures are not only in our own homes, but more specifically, under our own beds—buried deep within our essence. The search for external treasures is not only bound to fail, but may even prevent us from finding the treasures that are under our own beds.

If we are wise, we call on luck from within and not from some external source. Any external source of luck would have to run parallel to the determinations of the Greater Force of this universe. If this were true, then luck would be external to the Market. And this is not the case.

Wise people use the treasure "under their beds" to open a window and convert currency from one dimension to the other. And as if by miracle . . . a bissale mazel, a little luck, appears! Where does it come from? From the treasure hidden under the bed.

We must realize, though, that there can be no real gain in luck, because the resources are only being transferred from one world to another. If we keep this in mind, our relationship towards luck changes. Luck can be fruitful if it compensates a lack, but it's a waste if it brings surplus. Those who are wise know this and don't wish for luck as a means of accumulating. Anyone who works in the Market knows that accumulating can be very expensive. Accumulating means storage costs, the possibility of spoilage, and the depreciation of the product because it loses liquidity. Luck is like cash, and it's always good to have a little circulating capital in our lives.

The Talmud tells a story about Rabbi Ḥanina which emphasizes the attention we should give to our investments. Because Rabbi Ḥanina was a very poor man, and well known for his access to Heaven, he was challenged by his wife. "Ḥanina, since you are known as a man whose prayers are heard in Heaven, why don't you do something to overcome our misery? Why don't you ask for some money?"

"But we are very rich," answered Ḥanina, quite confidently.

"Yes, I know," retorted his wife, "but how about making a few withdrawals once in a while?"

Moved by his wife's request, Ḥanina prayed. His wish was granted, and a hand came down from Heaven bearing a table leg made of solid gold. The object was worth enough money to support them for the rest of their lives.

However, that night Ḥanina had a dream. He dreamed that he was in the celestial palace where the just men of all times were gathered around the Divine Presence. Each one sat at a table made of gold. In fact, they were three-legged golden tables. Ḥanina then realized that his table had only two legs.

When he woke up, he told his wife about the dream. They both agreed that he should pray to have the object returned. Again a hand came down from Heaven and took back the golden leg.

The rabbis comment that the second miracle was greater than the first, because the future is easier to change than the past.

What the rabbis are really saying is that it is easier to turn cash into a specific good than to reverse the process and turn the good back into "cash." It is best to keep luck in its convertible state than to summon it in trying to settle debts that could be settled in their own material dimension.

There is one kind of real gain in luck. It is a gain that is measured not in resources, but in awareness. Luck helps us to notice the existence of these parallel worlds of wealth. The great plus is that it surprises us. And we all need to be surprised in order to open our hearts to these other dimensions. This is the importance of a bissale mazel.

In Exodus 7:9, we are told of God's instruction to Moses as to how to approach Pharaoh and demand his people's freedom from slavery in Egypt: "When Pharaoh shall speak to you, saying, 'Show a sign for yourselves,' then say to Aaron, 'Cast your staff down and it will become a serpent.'" The commentators realized what a strange sentence this was. Shouldn't Pharaoh say, "Show a sign for *me*" and not "for yourselves"? But the rabbis themselves answer: "No, Pharaoh's challenge is correct. In order to test the real power of Moses, he wishes to know if Moses can perform a miracle that will surprise even himself."

When a magician performs his tricks, there is no better demonstration of power than when he manages to surprise himself. After all, what's special about the trick that we already know we can do? Being able to surprise yourself shows great power. And this is the real gain we derive from luck.

When we surprise ourselves, we awaken to discover our own treasures. And as Rabbi Nahman used to say, "May you make use of your treasures." In these uses, in these investments, no amount of caution is too much.

Angels

Our observations on luck are an expansion upon the idea of interconnection between everything and everyone. In other words, what we call good and bad luck is nothing but the wealth or scarcity of other worlds as interpreted from a material standpoint. And when we fail to fully understand this interconnection, we are faced with unexpected situations that we call luck. That's why, when we least expect it, we are shaken by coincidences and synchronicities that intrigue us. These "coincidences" are situations of this dimension that rise into higher dimensions and are influenced by them. And when they return to this dimension, they apparently reflect a discontinuity between cause and effect. This discontinuity fascinates us, especially as it conceals a relationship between events that we can't seem to grasp. An objectively random event becomes mysterious when we realize how appropriately it seems to fit our reality. Surprises of this kind have always happened. Human experience, however, impoverishes reality to such an extent that when we spot one of these "mysteries," we are astonished. The interconnection between the various worlds, which we don't often notice, is responsible for these astonishing manifestations.

Among these manifestations are angels (in Hebrew, *malakhim;* singular, *malakh:* literally, messenger or agent). Angels are connecting elements between the various worlds. They are not beings, but "motivations" that control people, situations, or opportunities. They are the messengers of what we call good and bad luck in the world of Asiyyah.

Rabbinical tradition (*Genesis Rabbah* 50:2) says that "an angel is never in charge of more than one mission, just as two angels are never in charge of the same mission." Each motivation is sent from one world to another towards a specific destination, because they were called upon from our dimension. In other words, any one of us could be seized by one of these motivations and become a messenger, a facilitator between worlds. Without noticing it, we are led to do things. We introduce certain people, or draw them towards opportunities, or because of something we do, someone is at a certain place at a certain time. How many times are we puzzled at someone's special affection for us because we've been instrumental in their life? And sometimes we don't even recall the situation that the person considers so significant. What happens is that we are part of the interconnections of this universe, and as such we become agents of luck, either good or bad. We are made into angels and fulfill our mission by mediating these motivations.

Motivations range from segulah to zekhut (merit), and they may load us with plenty or confirm our lacks. In a Ḥasidic tale, the Keretzer Rabbi said, "When we help someone, we create the angel called Azriel [literally, Helper of God]. When we contribute to tzedakah [justice], we create the angel called Tzadkiel [literally, Justice-maker of God]."

When we are aware of these interconnections, we send up to other worlds intentions that will later come back as motivations. If we pay attention, we realize that these intentions are already motivations in this dimension. But it's only when they come back to us as angels, affecting us directly, that we notice their presence—to our great surprise.

This is the most frightening element of our reality. We discover that we are not always heading where we think we are, or for the reasons we believed. We are much more intensely interactive than we imagined. This is such a dangerous insight that those who delve too deeply into it may experience emotional disturbances. The extent of our interactive essence is extremely disturbing to our sense of ego boundaries. But if on the one hand this realization unsettles us, on the other it makes for true understanding of certain Market and life processes.

After all, at the very center of the net of interaction lies the Fair Price, which is the absolute value of something. Each such price is responsible for the generation of an entire market. And there is no other way to have access to these prices but through our interactions. Prices are nothing but the products of interaction!

In the business world, the world of *gesheft*, these motivations circulate in abundance. They are the very motivations that surface as livelihood in our day-to-day interactions. We create constant opportunities for ourselves and for others by acting as angels, messengers of livelihood. Just as some birds pollinate plants, we participate in the fertilization of numerous processes of livelihood.

I have insisted, thus far, that wealth is an element not only of the material dimension. Angels must, therefore, be very careful in transporting things from one dimension to another. We must bear in mind that an angel can work towards enrichment or impoverishment, and the following Hasidic tale illustrates this:

The Rabbi of Rimanov dreamed that he had risen to the Heavens and overheard an angel asking God to allow him to bring riches down to the people. The angel was saying, "See how pious your people are, and what misery they live in. Give them riches and they will be even more dedicated to You."

The rabbi then asked who this angel was and was told that his name was Satan. The rabbi immediately exclaimed, "Leave us in poverty, O Eternal One! Save us from the favors of Satan!"

The Rimanover knew that livelihood and wealth don't always result from favorable interconnections. Often we are messengers of motivations that bring about bad consequences. When this happens, we become messengers of Satan, bearing obstacles to a richer life. Each gain, each piece of luck, each moment of livelihood should come to us without feelings of doubt or ambivalence. If this is not the case, we should suspect that we may be carrying obstacles to wealth instead of messages of livelihood.

8

OBSTACLES TO

WEALTH

The "Other Side" *(sitrah aḥarah)* is the name Jewish tradition gives to that which is evil. But we do not consider it an independent entity. As its name indicates, it is the *other* side. The Hebrew word *satan*, usually translated "adversary," could also be translated to mean "side effect." When looked at from the human point of view, the evil side effects of life don't seem to be random. They are the obstacles we face in life and that we feel were planted there intentionally. So smart is their disposition that we even imagine that there is an intelligent strategist behind them. This intelligence, however, is part of the nature of the Other Side, the shadow side of our physical and material experiences. The more complex life is, the more we have to lose, the more intense the Other Side is. The more intense the

light, the sharper the shadow, which is the effect of matter when exposed to light. This is one of the difficulties
of being or residing in a body. For millennia, religion
has emphasized that we are prisoners of our material
world. Because the concrete world demands that we
comprehend all that we see through this perspective,
we try to transform everything into "things" and recognize only material reality. When we look at colors, for
example, what we are seeing is not an absolute property
of an object, but the way in which light and radiation
affect our eyes. Everything we perceive about matter is
an ephemeral manifestation destined to disappear as a
result of the finitude of life itself. And the possibility of
"loss" that we must endure in the material world is part
of the same reality as "owning"—it is its other side.

We cannot exorcise this other side from our material world. This is why spirituality is so important, because things related to the spirit have no "other side."
What belongs to the soul and to spiritual growth casts
no shadow and is a form of "having" without fear of
loss. This is our divine aspect, our "image and likeness," which we shall never lose, not even in death.

This is why prosperity is such a complicated condition. If we are quite honest, we must admit that wealth
does not relieve us of the agonies and contradictions of
the material world. In a sense, there is no difference
between wealth and poverty. It's obvious that misery is
a destructive evil because it keeps us from participating
in the Market and its incredible opportunities. But poverty, which is also a physical condition of matter, only

refers to one dimension of the Market. Like the colors we see, "rich" and "poor" are only perceptions we apprehend using our bodily apparatus.

Even though wealth represents no extra advantage over poverty in the other worlds, it can be a great obstacle to wealth in these other dimensions.

The Rabbi of Chernobyl used to say, "Between poverty and wealth, I have always chosen poverty. It's the best protection against miserliness and weaknesses of the spirit. It's cheap and easy to buy. Therefore, it's a good deal. If we are poor, we need not fight desperately against envy and competition. We answer to no one and need not deal with suspicion. And people understand us without our having to justify or explain ourselves. I beg you, my friends, don't deprive me of this treasure!"

Wealth is a difficult thing. It confronts us constantly with the ephemeral nature of life, disguises our moments of descent on the wheel, and sometimes causes us to lose a great deal of time. I am not eulogizing poverty. The rabbis are clear on this point: increasing the wealth of the world is a commandment. Yet we are warned to treat every moment of fortune with caution, because it can become a great obstacle to true wealth. If you are prospering, first I wish you "Mazel tov!" (Congratulations!), and then I recommend that you seek help. First of all, enjoy, and immediately afterwards, try to balance your wealth in the different worlds. One of the tools through which you can do this is tzedakah.

The Rabbi of Tsechiv commented on the priestly blessing with which God commanded Aaron and his descendants to bless the Israelites (Numbers 6:24): "May the Lord bless you and safeguard you." The rabbi asked, "Why 'bless' and 'safeguard'? When we are blessed, do we not have everything? Often wealth brings with it evil things, and this is why the priests blessed people with these words. They wanted us to be blessed with wealth and at the same time protected from it."

This commentary helps us to understand one of the more complex things in life. There is a constant partnership between this world and other worlds, between human beings and the Divine. Blessings are not divine grace. Nor are they the fulfillment of our human expectations about life. It is in the "safeguarding" that we see the link between Heaven and earth. In keeping the doors open to higher worlds, we experience faith and hope. We want not simply to wait for these doors to open and pour down blessings upon us, but to learn to unlock the doors to an investment Market that is much larger than the one that we see in this material dimension.

Safeguarding is therefore the complement of blessing, and doesn't mean that you are special or "loved" by God. When we are systematically blessed, we sometimes fall into the trap of believing ourselves to be special. How many of us use our material blessings to concoct a vision of the world that is an obstacle to real wealth? Take some time to ponder this Hasidic parable, which tries to explain why wicked people sometimes seem to receive more blessings than righteous people:

> It is like a King who has two sons. Each son comes to the royal banquet to receive a gift.
>
> The first son need only come to the door of the hall, and his wish is granted. The father has little love for this son, and his very presence bothers him. The King orders that his requests be granted at the door so that he need not come up to the table.
>
> Next comes the favorite son. The father takes great pleasure in his arrival and doesn't want him to leave so quickly. This is why he delays granting his requests, hoping that his son will come even closer to him. When the son comes closer, he senses the extent of his father's love for him, and he isn't reluctant even to serve himself from the banquet table.

If only those who are blessed realized the favor of being safeguarded, of serving themselves from the table itself. Those who are safeguarded by God stroll through the other worlds, discovering other Markets and investing in them. We might even imagine an ascending scale of values for blessing and safeguarding that would help us to understand the possible investments we could make with our blessings so that they result also in divine protection. The accompanying table shows possible investments in the various worlds.

So these are the investments: In the material

	Blessings in . . .	*May Safeguard . . .*
World	*Wealth*	*Investment*
ATZILUT Emanation	LISHMAH "For its own sake" No representation in wealth	STUDY, LEARNING
BERIAH Creation	ZEKHUT Merit	KEDOSHIM TIHIU Being Holy
YETZIRAH Foundation	SEGULAH Treasure	GEMILUT ḤASADIM Acts of Kindness
ASIYYAH Action	NEKHES Material Goods	TZEDAKAH Responsible Taxing

world, we work towards the settlement and enrichment of the world through tzedakah and the responsible taxing of transactions. If we do this, we increase *nekhes,* property. In the world of emotions, the investment is in *gemilut ḥasadim,* acts of kindness towards others. Gemilut ḥasadim are different from tzedakah. Tzedakah is justice, and without it our money contains theft. Gemilut ḥasadim are acts of "charity." They are gestures that reflect a concern for others born of a projection of our love for our neighbor and our identification with him or her. Gemilut ḥasadim open the doors of the emotional world and increase the treasures that are available to us in moments of need.

In the world of the spirit, the investment is in *kedoshim tihiu*. This is the biblical expression that exhorts us all to become "priests," or, as the expression reads: "Be holy, for I am holy" (Leviticus 11:45). The word *holy* in Hebrew, *kadosh*, comes from the root meaning "to separate." Making something holy or sacred means differentiating it from other things. This investment requires that we go beyond primitive normative ethics and behave based on the ethics of a *tzaddik* (righteous person). In the dimension of holiness, it isn't even necessary to identify directly with the other person—you don't love the other because he or she could be you; you simply internalize this love for every living thing and for all that interact. But you can deal with the differences in such a special way that you begin to operate as if everything were sacred. At this level, we no longer experience loss, and when we experience gain, it is in the form of zekhut, merit. This is where we cross the boundary into what we can take from this world.

The world of Emanation, on the other hand, is referred to by the rabbis as "the empty space where there is no longer right or left," and in it there is no gain. There was no loss in the previous level, and there is no gain here either. This is the world of *lishmah*, where things are done for their own sake. In this world, there are no rewards, there is no enrichment, no manifestation of livelihood. And at the same time, all the other worlds are under the constant influence of this dimension.

In the world of Emanation we do not interact with

others as if they were differentiated from ourselves in an absolute way, and because of this there's no merit whatsoever involved. In this dimension where there is no *other*, where everything is one, all transactions involve studying. The Torah—the Testament—represents an investment that came to us from higher worlds and was for us a great revelation. Not a revelation in words or in content, but above all in the concept of studying *lishmah*—studying for no purpose other than learning itself.

There's a story of a rabbi who was allowed to enter the world-to-come. At first, he was disappointed because he had expected to find a grand place where the righteous lived in luxury, surrounded by wonders. All he found was people studying in a celestial yeshiva (school). So he asked, "Is that what they do here? Isn't that what they did during their life on earth?" And the answer came, "Yes. But now they *understand* what they study!"

In the world-to-come, studying and understanding are the same thing. In this dimension there is no Other Side, because all sides merge into one.

9

DEATH AND WEALTH: CAN YOU TAKE IT WITH YOU?

We have seen that in the dimension of holiness we can accumulate wealth that does not have an Other Side to it. In other words, we can suffer no loss. And because of this, these are riches that can follow us even beyond this dimension. In fact, they are not material belongings at all, if that makes any sense.

Think it over. Many people imagine that having cash is good. In a way, this seems true, because with cash we can open up many possibilities of "having." However, the wise investor disagrees with this. Cash is not an investment, but a withdrawal on investment. Cash is only momentary livelihood. A clear example of this was the manna that God caused to fall from the skies in the correct portion every day. Those who tried to gather more than their daily share were snatching someone else's possibilities while the portion they stored rotted. It's the same way with money in the form of coins—it rots. Because of this, we must work towards our future livelihood and invest in things that don't spoil. If we do, we'll end up owning things that are not possessions, but expectations of ownership that we invest in, hoping that they will one day become possessions.

And what are the possible investments? We can invest in other people's vitality, in their creativity. We can bet on their luck or their organization. We can invest in food or energy production, or in commodities of all kinds. All these options are part of the manna offered to us every day by the market. The rabbis believed that cash could also be stored in the form of interactions. To them, some of our best investments, those more resistant to decay, are the ones that we obtain through being holy.

In the Bible, there is a very special passage that contains the secret from which we derive many of the questions we have discussed so far. The Ten Commandments are a list of "investments" that we should make in order to gather dividends from community life. And there's a similarly important passage known as *Kedoshim* (Holy Things). In this passage (Leviticus 19–20) we find commandments aimed at the righteous, the hidden secrets of how to "invest" in order to draw livelihood from the greater Society, which encompasses all those who are alive now, were alive in the past, and will live in the future. A story told in the Talmud (*Bava Batra* 11a) presents an example of someone who was aware of the return on such investments:

During a period of famine, King Monobaz [an emperor who converted to Judaism in the first century] gave away the entire fortune he had received from his parents. His brothers and other relatives protested, saying, "You are giving away not only your money, but the money you inherited from your ancestors." He answered, "My ancestors gathered treasures down here, but I gather them in Heaven, because it is written: *Truth will sprout from the earth and righteousness will come down from the Heavens to the earth* [Psalms 85:12].

"My ancestors stored treasures where they could be stolen by human hands. But I store them where no hands can get at them, because it is written: *Righteousness and Justice are the foundation of Your throne* [Psalms 89:15].

"My ancestors stored treasures that today they receive no interest for, and I store them so that they will give interest, because it is written: *It shall be well with the righteous, for they shall eat the fruits of their work!* [Isaiah 3:10].

"My ancestors stored their money in safes, and I store mine in souls that have been saved, because it is written: *The fruit* [cash] *of the righteous is a tree of life, and all who win souls* [who will testify in their favor] *are wise* [Proverbs 11:30].

"My ancestors stored treasures for their descendants, and I store them for myself, because it is written: *For you justice must be credited before God* [Deuteronomy 24:13].

"My ancestors stored treasures in this world, but I store them in the world-to-come, because it is written: *Your justice shall march before you* [to intercede on your behalf in the world-to-come] [Isaiah 58:8]."

We must learn from the Market, so as to be true creatures of *gesheft,* how to invest and save in all dimensions. If we spend our time here collecting only goods of a material nature, we won't be able to carry them with us to the next stop, because the only thing we know about the next stop is that it doesn't grant entrance to anything material. The body that remains here, like an empty shell, holds on to everything that pertained to it. If you dedicate all your efforts to this, beware! You will carry little luggage.

The Rabbi of Mezeritz used to tell the following story:

A king sent his two sons to a distant country to learn about its culture and finance. On the way, their ship wrecked and they arrived with nothing. The two princes began to work for a living, and all they earned, they spent on maintaining themselves. One of the princes made a great effort to live a simple life so that he would still have time to study the culture and economics of the country. The other prince worked only to pay his own expenses. Sometime later, the first prince returned to his father with many novelties and much knowledge. The second prince also returned, but he was unable to bring his riches with him. This prince returned with little knowledge and empty hands, and he got no attention from his father.

The princes represent the souls that are sent to this world to collect knowledge and acts of kindness. If we are smart, we won't waste all our efforts in this world with "unprofitable" activities and will make an effort to bring back many novelties. Only the fool returns empty-handed.

Those who understand this look for an exchange rate for their potentialities that will allow them to live a life of holiness. This is why the good *gesheft*, the good deal, aims not only at our own livelihood, but also at generating livelihood for all those interacting. In this dimension we are responsible for everything that we become aware of. And the more we see, the more responsible we are. This is a very costly attitude, because in order to discover ways of circulating between the various worlds, we must find ways of surrendering to and trusting the Market. And this is extremely difficult!

Rabbi Uri explained a legend that describes how Abraham, when young, refused to bow to idols and as a punishment was thrown into the fire. But, incredible though it may seem, he didn't burn: "Abraham thought, 'If I want the idols to be thrown into the fire, I must be thrown into the fire myself.' This is why he survived.

His brother Haran, however, when he saw that nothing had happened to Abraham, jumped into the fire too and was burned alive."

Our idols are so deeply rooted that the only way we can purify ourselves is by walking into the fire. This is an internal process that Abraham knew well, and he knew that it isn't enough just to recognize your idols; it is necessary to throw them into the fire. Idols are our attachments to this material world—the concrete sticks and stones of physical existence. And fire is the capacity to evaluate prices and costs simultaneously in all worlds: material, emotional, intellectual, and spiritual. This is how we acquire circulating money, cash that has real value and can be converted into currency in all worlds.

When we internalize idols, we are impoverishing ourselves in a very real way. Therefore, we should be very careful in our daily activities that aim at livelihood in the material world. In dealing with this world we may take on so many unexpected costs that our business fails to generate any real profit. The Baal Shem Tov warned about this danger by making the following comparison:

"When a diver dives into the ocean looking for pearls, he must hold his breath and concentrate on his task. This is what we should do when we dive into the material world looking for Torah [holiness]. We should be careful not to lose our sense of the sacred and be seduced by things. Because if this happens, the pressure will destroy our spiritual life, in the same way that the pressure of the water can kill a distracted diver."

In order to be careful divers, we must understand that we take a lot with us. We should try to act like we would in the earthly Market. We know that great investors often invest in foreign banks as protection against destabilization in their own country. In the same way, we should not keep all our life capital in only one "currency"—especially if it is an investment in something as ephemeral as our own life. If we invest only in ourselves, we will lose all our riches when we die. But if we realize that we need not invest only in ourselves, the opportunities of the Market increase tenfold. To make this kind of investment, we must begin by discovering the other—our neighbor, the closest person to us in this universe. Investing in others we go beyond the limitations on what we can take with us from this world. Our neighbor is our first goal in trying to join with the One. He or she is the key to canceling the influence of the Other Side, because when we identify with our neighbor, the external element becomes a part of us, and all "sides" come together as one.

The Book of Proverbs (27:19) says: "Like the face in the water that reflects another face, the heart of one person answers the heart of another." The rabbinical commentators ask, "Why water and not a mirror?" And they answer: "Because in order to see oneself in the water, one must kneel and come close to it." And what is proximity if it's not a *gesheft*, a business and an interaction? It is in this very day-to-day Market of exchanges that we invest in other worlds and in the Greater Market. From our daily acts spring constant deposits to our savings accounts in nonmaterial worlds. These are the worlds that interact with our world and the places where we will set up residence when we are no longer material beings.

May we be inscribed in the Book of Livelihood and enjoy a positive balance that will allow us to operate on the Market for all time.

10

MONEY IN THE
WORLD-TO-COME

There is a story about a king who sent for a peasant, who was very frightened at this summons. He prepared himself and set off towards the palace. His friends, out of solidarity, accompanied him to the walls of the village, and his family went with him up to the palace doors. From there onwards, only the peasant's merits and his ability to take care of himself would follow him.

The rabbis consider this a parable of life. Someday we will be called to the palace. "This world is like a corridor into the world-to-come; prepare yourself in the corridor so that you may enter the banquet hall" (*Ethics of the Fathers* 4:21). Our belongings and our property—which are here called "friends"—will follow us until the outskirts of the village. In other words, we can enjoy them until our last breath. Our family will follow us until our burial, the entrance to the palace, but they go no farther. Into the palace, and into the banquet hall, only our good deeds can follow.

When we face the King, we bring only the choices we made for life, our good deals, which are converted into credit.

Up until recently, the only apparatus available to measure and evaluate this aspect of our lives was pragmatic intuition: "Be 'good' and later this will bring you rewards." In our time, ecology has been a small and at the same time a huge step towards providing better resources for this evaluation. There is a Market of interconnection where certain attitudes are "good" or not. I refer to attitudes supporting a system that wishes to be supported versus attitudes that threaten this system. There is something beyond pleasure and escape from pain that is just as important. It's as if we've discovered a real interest outside our own bodies, outside ourselves.

The rabbis saw this. Not because they had magic, but because they understood the lens through which we look at things. They used to say that when you look at glass, you can see right through it. Put a little silver on the glass and it turns into a mirror, so that the only thing we see is ourselves. With a little money, what was once transparent becomes immediately obscure and we can no longer tap into any external reality.

The learned men of Israel believed that there are only three ways to tap into this dimension beyond matter, and see through glass and not a mirror. Study, prayer, and good deeds are the three processes that refer us from our material world to a higher dimension.

If we overlook the vulgarization that these words have suffered over the years, we will realize that they are the tools we use to track down other dimensions and other realities. The late Professor Saul Liberman of the Jewish Theological Seminary used to say that prayer is when we speak to the Creator, and study is when the Creator speaks to us. Our meditations, the way we look up at the skies, our rituals, our prayers uttered in solitude—all this reflects our belief that there is something behind the mirror. When we study the traditions and the teachings distilled in each generation as it looked beyond the mirror, we are collecting messages from a medium that has been made transparent for us.

Good attitudes that are life-affirming (*le-ḥayyim*, for life) are those that take the other, our neighbor, into consideration and transcend our individual bodies. These attitudes are the limits of our materiality. If we internalize every moment through a good *gesheft*, we will be looking at life using glass and not a mirror, so that nothing separates us from the experience itself. This is difficult to grasp, especially as we come closer to death and to surrendering all our worldly belongings. Ḥasidic masters used to say: "In our last three hours before the world-to-come it is as difficult to hang on to life as it is to climb a wall of ice. This is why we repeat the words 'Help us in the three hours' in our prayers."

The rabbis' emphasis on good deals teaches us that it is easier to reach understanding through behavior than to modify behavior based on understanding. So, if our main occupation in the world-to-come will be studying, listening directly to the Creator, and understanding, the important thing while we're here is to be constantly involved in good *gesheftn* or else studying to be free to practice them more frequently. Good deals fill us with hope and make livelihood our most direct connection to faith.

What is behavior here is consciousness later on. Money here is study and comprehension later on.

And when I say money, I mean the real money generated in good *gesheftn*. Money for the sake of money itself is not really circulating currency; it's just an illusion, a phenomenon of the mirror.

> Rabbi Yosef, son of Rabbi Yoshua ben Levy, was very sick and fell into a coma. When he got better, his father asked, "What did you see?"
> "I saw a world upside down, a misty world where everything was inverted," he answered. "The greatest people on earth were the lowliest there, and the lowliest people on earth were the highest there."
> "My son," said the father, "you didn't see a misty world, you saw a very clear world."
> *(Pesaḥim* 50a)

It's time to reconsider your savings account, and even the nature of your business. Look carefully at the needs of the Market around you.

Jews, because of the persecutions they suffered

and because they often had to flee their homes, took care never to have their money immobilized. Who knew? They might have to leave town at any moment. Some chose dollars or jewels to invest in. But those who understand the parable of their experience in this world keep their capital completely realizable. They have their money readily available through "true interactions" that they conduct in their lives and in moments in which they fulfill the commandment to be holy. So, when they have to leave, they won't arrive at the other shore empty-handed. They'll have at least the minimum necessary to set up a small business in the world-to-come, draw their livelihood from it, and—who knows?—even prosper.

Completed in the year 5751 of the Jewish calendar,
during the week in which we read in the synagogue
the passage that says:
Kedoshim tihiu ki kadosh ani YHVH Eloheikhem.
You must be holy because I am God your Lord,
and I am holy.
(Leviticus 19:2)

Bibliography

Buber, Martin. *Ten Rungs.* New York: Schocken Books, 1947.

―――. *Historias do Rabi.* São Paulo: Editora Perspectiva, 1967.

Disho, David. *Tarbut ha-Machloket be-Yisrael.* Tel Aviv: Schocken Books, 1984.

Feinsilver, Alexander. *Talmud for Today.* New York: St. Martin's Press, 1980.

Goldin, Hyman. *Ethics of the Fathers.* New York: Hebrew Publishing Company, 1962.

Kantor, Mattis. *Guide to the Entangled.* New York: Naran Chai Publications, 1990.

Kaplan, Aryeh, trans. *The Living Torah.* New York: Maznaim, 1981.

Klagsbrun, Francine. *Voices of Wisdom.* New York: Pantheon, 1980.

Kushner, Lawrence. *Honey from the Rock.* Woodstock, N.Y.: Jewish Lights Publishing, 1990.

Leibowitz, Nehama. *Studies in the Bible.* Jerusalem: Ahva Press, 1980.

Levine, Aaron. *Free Enterprise and Jewish Law.* New York: Ktav Publishing House/Yeshiva University Press, 1980.

BIBLIOGRAPHY

Lipman, Eugene. *Mishna.* New York: Norton and Company, 1970.

Montefiore, C. G., and H. Loewe. *Rabbinic Anthology.* New York: Schocken Books, 1988.

Nachman of Bratslav, Rabbi. *Garden of the Souls.* New York: Breslov Research Institute, 1990.

Neusner, Jacob. *Tzedaka.* New York: Rossel Books, 1982.

Newman, Louis. *Hasidic Anthology.* New York: Schocken Books, 1963.

Rosten, Leo. *Treasury of Jewish Quotations.* New York: Mc-Graw-Hill, 1972.

Schachter-Shalomi, Zalman. *Paradigm Shift: From the Jewish Renewal Teachings of Reb Zalman Schachter-Shalomi.* Edited by Ellen Singer. Northvale, N.J.: Jason Aronson, 1993.

———, with Donald Gropman. *The First Step: A Guide for the New Jewish Spirit.* New York: Bantam Books, 1983.

———, and Edward Hoffman. *Sparks of Light.* Boulder, Colo.: Shambhala Publications, 1983.

Schwartz, Richard. *Judaism and Global Survival.* New York: Atara Publishing, 1987.

Siegel, Danny. *Where Heaven and Earth Touch.* New York: Town House Press, 1983.

Tamari, Meir. *With All Your Possessions.* New York: Free Press, 1987.

Tanakh. Philadelphia: Jewish Publication Society, 1985.